A HIDDEN WORLD

A Hidden World

BY RAPHAEL RUPERT

EDITED BY *Anthony Rhodes*

INTRODUCTION BY *Edward Crankshaw*

THE WORLD PUBLISHING COMPANY

CLEVELAND AND NEW YORK

Published by The World Publishing Company
2231 West 110th Street, Cleveland 2, Ohio

Library of Congress Catalog Card Number: 63-8775

FIRST EDITION

MWP

AN UNCOMMON VALOR REPRINT EDITION
Printed in the United States of America

ISBN: 9798869042279

Introduction by Edward Crankshaw

The first thing to be said is that this is a true story. I had the privilege of meeting Mr. Rupert when he finally escaped from Hungary in the autumn of 1956 and was still too dazed to talk much about his Russian experiences. But it was then at once clear that he was a man of exceptional honesty and that anything he cared later to say about his life in Soviet labour camps would be of especial value because of this. And so, I think, it turns out to be.

In writing of what he lived through in the hands of the Soviet political police he has not been tempted, as a more imaginative, more self-conscious individual would have been tempted, to strive for effect or to generalise from his personal experience, or even by meditating aloud on causes and effects to blur the particular image of what happened to him. Although he had already had glimpses of Soviet reality under Stalin he had no clear picture of what he would have to suffer and when he was finally sentenced to twenty-five years' forced labour, on a trumped-up charge of espionage for the British, he went off on that appalling prison train as on a voyage of discovery. Indeed, one of the most fascinating aspects of his story is the Man-from-Mars view of the dark side of a continent.

It should not be thought that Mr. Rupert had no standpoint of his own. On the contrary, his standpoint was so firm that he took it completely for granted. It was that of the convinced, instinctive liberal individualist.

His father was a distinguished Liberal politician, and he himself had hoped to follow the family tradition. But the war came and, in lieu of politics, Mr. Rupert turned his hand to helping allied airmen and Jews to escape from the Germans. This seemed to him the most natural thing in the world. It was the "liberal" thing. Thus, when he told his Russian captors that he was a Liberal, and suffered terribly for it, what he really meant by Liberalism was simply the principle of freedom to be oneself. It is plain that even now he has not realised the massiveness of the forces working against this simple principle, and not only in Communist countries.

But even if I had never met Mr. Rupert I should have recognised at once the truth of his story. I should have had no doubt at all that everything happened to Mr. Rupert precisely as he has set it down, and it seemed to me that the value of the picture he builds up is all the greater because of the matter of fact limitations of his approach. It is this which gives a particular value too to Mr. Rupert's account of the last phase of his imprisonment and his final release some time after Stalin's death. We are here taken into the world of prison camps in the process of breaking up and receive remarkable insights into the Soviet way of doing things when good, not evil, is the aim. More than this, in the extraordinary, interesting record of Mr. Rupert's final interrogations in the Lubianka prison (now no longer as an accused, but as a witness for the prosecution of Beria's accomplices) we are given a glimpse from behind the scenes, which I think is unique, of the agonised process of de-Stalinisation as it affected the apparatus of police terror.

For the rest, Mr. Rupert has simply told from day to day over a period of eight years what happened when an ordinary, unassuming Central European found himself caught up in the insane ferocity of ideological warfare.

It began when he was arrested in Budapest in 1947, and the reader will note with interest that he received more malignant personal violence at the hands of his fellow-countrymen, acting as Rakosi's policemen, than during all his enforced stay in Russia. It continued when he was removed to Baden, the enchanting Habsburg spa in the wooded hills just outside Vienna, which the Russians chose as their Austrian Potsdam. And for me his descriptions of what went on during his imprisonment and interrogation, which ended in a false confession and a twenty-five years' sentence in this cosy little holiday town, almost within visual signalling distance of the Allied occupation forces in Vienna itself, a morsel of the old Europe if ever there was one, has a special fascination which is not surpassed by any of the experiences, horrifying and macabre, which were to follow on the long train journey to Russia and in the labour camps themselves. No doubt this is because I knew more about the labour camps than I knew about the interior of Marshal Malinovski's idyllic Austrian headquarters!

Others will, I expect, be more interested by the insights offered by Mr. Rupert into aspects of the Soviet way of life.

It is these that I can vouch for. I have never been inside a Soviet labour camp, but a number of my friends, chiefly Russian, have shared the sort of life described by Mr. Rupert and some have lived to talk about it. Further, at one time and another, I myself have had close-up views of forced labour in action. There was a time, during and soon after the war, when life was at such a low ebb throughout the Soviet Union that in the remote areas—and in some areas not so remote—it was often impossible to tell a free citizen from a prisoner. Certain northern landscapes seemed to be nothing but a Paul Nash nightmare of geometrically arranged fences of barbed wire—fences punctuated by watch-towers on stilts, with machine-guns and searchlights, the guards heavily, stiffly cocooned in goatskin *shubas* nearly down to the ground so that they looked like wigwams; there were the prisoners, being marched about, or doing fatigues, or man-handling heavy timber, or trying to break up frozen soil and sub-soil to sink foundations. And next to them came free labourers, with nothing in their appearance or the work they were doing to show the difference. Nobody cared: they were all half dead of hunger anyway. I have seen—I have told this elsewhere —gangs of prisoners from a camp in North Russia laying strategic railways, building new wharves, breaking up the ice laboriously with broken tools at forty degrees below zero centigrade—and alongside them there have been gangs of free citizens, "volunteers," doing the same work, and marching back at the end of their shift to communal barracks. Many of these were girls. I have seen the sort of swift public copulations described by Mr. Rupert. And I have had fall dead at my feet a prisoner shot by a guard for falling out of line to pick up a crust of bread thrown from the galley of an iced-up merchant ship— and seen how the corpse was left lying like a dead cat in a slum street, until after a few days there was nothing to be seen but a faint hummock under sifted snow.

This sort of action was not cruelty, but the outcome of total callousness and stupidity, itself produced by the policies of Stalin, coming on top of Lenin and centuries of Tsarist brutality. You cannot, agreed, make an omelette without breaking eggs, as Lenin with his ineffable brightness once remarked. But it took Lenin to produce a situation in which, with manic hopefulness, men break eggs by the bucketful—and then find that there is no frying-pan, no match to light the fire and nobody around who knows how to make an omelette . . .

This is the kind of mood which has to be realised before Mr. Rupert's story can be understood. Then think back. Think back to Dostoievsky's *House of the Dead*, to Chekhov's *Sakhalin Island*, to Gogol's *Dead Souls*. All the violence, venality, squalor, degradation and sheer *waste* of human resources exist in these books from before the revolution. The privileged murderers and thieves who terrorised the camps under Stalin, Mr. Rupert's "bandits," were at it in Dostoievsky's time, encouraged by Authority, which regarded political offenders as being far more wicked and dangerous than the most brutal criminals. The mindless brutality of the professional camp guards, the corruption and sycophancy of the camp authorities—all these go back to long before 1917. So, even, do the prison vans which made up Mr. Rupert's terrible trainloads of deportees: they were the proud invention of a Tsarist prime minister, Stolypin, who was himself assassinated while attending a gala performance opera in Kiev. Although Mr. Rupert did not know this, the vans are still called after him.

Having dwelt on the worst, let us look at the other side of the picture. One of the few encouraging developments at an extremely discouraging moment of history has been the improvement during the past few years of living conditions, material and moral, in the Soviet Union. This has been in certain ways so marked that there are already many people who think that we should forget the past and dwell only on the present and the future. I do not refer here to Communists and fellow-travellers who refused to recognise the evils of Stalinism until they were instructed to do so by Stalin's successor. These are past salvation. I refer, rather, to all sorts of well-meaning men and women who, while freely admitting that evil once reigned throughout that vast, unhappy land, nevertheless persuade themselves that no purpose is served by "raking up" past iniquities upon which the present leadership has turned its back.

This attitude will not do. In the first place it is treacherous: a betrayal of the memories of millions of fellow human beings who died and suffered inconceivably, unknown and unoffending—in order that Stalin could build up the power to dominate half Europe and to construct the "material base" from which Khrushchev could launch his sputniks. They must not be forgotten nor must those who made them suffer. Khrushchev has gone a long way towards apologising for the iniquity from which his improved model Soviet Union is arising, and he has gone still further in his efforts to ensure that such iniquity is not repeated. But in his denunciation of Stalin for his wholesale liquidation of faithful Communists and for his purges of the army command, he has not gone far enough. The great mass of the millions in Stalin's labour camps and prisons were not Communists at all: they were ordinary Soviet citizens needed for forced labour to open up the resources of the least habitable parts of the land; they were peasants who resisted the collectivisation; they were innocents denounced by informers and arrested by the political police as part of a régime of terror; they were the citizens of many lands overrun by the Soviet army and taken away to serve long terms in the interior, partly because they were needed for the vast slave labour enterprises of the MVD, partly again as an aspect of terror—Lithuanians, Latvians, Estonians, Poles, Czechs, Slovaks, Germans, Rumanians, Bulgarians, Yugoslavs, Austrians, and Hungarians like Mr. Rupert himself. Khrushchev has had nothing to say about these nameless, faceless millions, who had nothing to do with Communism, or with the domestic and foreign policies which produced victimisation on such a calamitous scale. Until books like Mr. Rupert's can be translated into Russian and published in Moscow it is our duty to remember what Khrushchev prefers to forget.

Further, how except by "raking up" the past can we hope to understand the present, which, everywhere—and not only in the Soviet Union—is the prisoner of the past? For the past is in the present, and from both the future springs.

Finally, it seems to me that the people who ask us to forgive and forget can never have understood the full enormity of what we are requested to forgive and forget. Mr. Rupert can show them something of this; and that is why I warmly commend his book.

Not that his story comes as a revelation. There have, over the years, been a very considerable number of reliable and highly instructive writings about life in Soviet prison camps, including at least two classics: Elinor Lipper's *Eleven Years in Soviet Prison Camps* and Gustav Herling's *Worlds Apart*. Indeed, there has long been no excuse for ignorance of what went on all over the Soviet Union until a very few years ago. But Mr. Rupert's book, as I have already said, seems to me to have a special value because of its extraordinary simplicity and unassumingness. Gustav Herling, Elinor Lipper and others in a lesser degree took their raw material as they found it and were above all concerned with exploring in their very different ways the problem of physical and spiritual survival in a wholly destructive world. They wanted to tell us something new about the human spirit, and they succeeded. But the trouble with classics is that by turning life into art, action into causes and consequences, and the particular into the universal, they offer a sort of catharsis, so that the impact of the everyday concrete is muffled. Instead of registering that such and such unspeakable events took place day after day, month after month, decade after decade, a jet flight away, just round the curvature of the earth, under our own familiar sun and moon and stars, and to human beings like us, we find ourselves wrapt in contemplation of the mysterious ways of the Almighty, seen in a grand historical perspective. Meanwhile individuals go on being hurt—and for no other reason but that some unspeakable dictator finds himself too inefficient to govern properly, and hits out savagely to cover up.

To try to appreciate and understand the Soviet Union of to-day without first contemplating the Russia of Mr. Rupert, so different from the Russia of, for example, Sir Charles Snow, is frivolous and vain. The thing to remember about the narrative which follows is that it is almost contemporary. It begins in 1947 and it ends in 1955. Six years ago Mr. Rupert, with millions of others, was still in a Soviet labour camp. Most of the camps are now closed; but, such is life in the Soviet Union, hundreds of thousands who were once prisoners and are now free, still live of their own volition (they have nowhere else to go) in and around the old camp hutments. Six years ago, although conditions were improving, the vast and intolerable network of the MVD's forced labour system still formed a vital part of the Soviet economic system. Six years ago conditions in many parts of the Union were still such that prisoners used to send food parcels from the camps to their relatives living as free peasants outside. The Soviet Union tested her first atom bomb in 1949, quite early on, in time, in Mr. Rupert's narrative. The first sputnik went up in 1952, when Mr. Rupert was still toiling away with, as far as he knew, more than twenty years of slavery ahead of him—he and millions of others. Seven years ago Mr. Rupert was at last sent home to Hungary (and the story of his long-drawn-out release is one of the most fascinating parts of the book) —only to be seized by the political police of his own native land—and to escape, by a miracle, during the Hungarian uprising of 1956. But during all these years we have been so obsessed with the evidences of Soviet technical skill, as applied to sputniks and nuclear fission, that we have allowed ourselves to be hypnotised into believing that the Soviet Union is peopled exclusively with budding Gagarins, Oistrakhs, Ulanovas and Botvinniks.

This misconception not only leads to a false idea of the state of the Soviet Union now, to-day; even worse, perhaps, it stands in the way of a proper appreciation of the vitality and the drive, the sheer magnitude of the effort now being applied to bring these people out of the abyss. In the first place, a moment's reflection will show that the Soviet Union cannot have utterly transformed itself in six years (ponder a little on the implications of Mr. Rupert's chapters about the furniture factory and the collective farm). In the second place, and more importantly I think, the fact that an oppressed and shattered people, which has known such depths of degradation and humiliation, and the corruption inseparable from it, can even begin to transform itself as the Soviet people are undeniably transforming themselves to-day, could, through the terrible years, keep the spark of humanity burning, to be fanned, when occasion offered, into a flame, carries for us all a supremely important message about the unquenchable vitality of the human spirit. Here, in these pages, is the almost unbelievable background to the newly emerging Soviet society, which has produced, together with the first *moujik* politician, Mr. Khrushchev, that host of clever and amiable diplomats, engineers, scientists, artists, writers, dancers, musicians and artisans who so fascinate us to-day. If this can happen, anything can happen. The problems confronting Russians working desperately and often misguidedly to escape from their own past make our own problems seem elementary and our own despondencies uncalled for.

Acknowledgements

Not long after I escaped from Hungary in 1956 I dictated my account of the previous nine years as a prisoner in Russia on to a tape-recorder. A friend kindly typed it in Hungarian for me.

I would like to thank Miss Evelyn Pinching and Mr. Paul Ignotus who, among others, were responsible for this script being translated into English. It comprised about half a million words, and I wish to thank also the translators—Mrs. Paul Ignotus, Mrs. Denise Gosztola, Mrs. Katalin Szasz, Mrs. Charlotte Erdos, Mr. Paul Hempton—for their work. The material was then edited and reassembled in its present, much reduced, form by Mr. Anthony Rhodes, to whom I am especially grateful.

R.R.

Contents

CONTENTS

WESTWARD
1954-1956

TO THE MEMORY OF MY FELLOW PRISONERS

I. EASTWARD

1947-1949

Arrest

On 17th November, 1956, I landed at Blackbushe aerodrome in Hampshire with the first batch of Hungarians to escape to England during the revolution.

A few days before I had been persuaded to leave Hungary, as I had only just been released after years of imprisonment in Russia and my friends were afraid that if the rising collapsed I might be given a further sentence on the suspicion that I had taken part in it. Everything had happened so quickly that I had not even had time to change my clothes and I was still wearing my Russian prison uniform when I landed on British soil.

At Blackbushe we were met by various officials who took us up to London and lodged us for the first few days in a hotel. Thereafter we were left to find our own feet and for the next few months the British authorities made no attempt to cross-question us or to find out if we could give them any useful information. This surprised me because after my experiences in Russia there were a number of valuable things I could have told them. However I discovered afterwards that this was the routine for dealing with political refugees. The security authorities preferred to leave them alone for some months (although keeping them under observation) to see if they approached, or were approached by, any suspicious characters. Once they were convinced that a man was a *bona fide* emigre, and would lead them to no espionage contacts, they would interview him.

After about seven months in England I was summoned to Whitehall. Although I had worked in an underground movement for the allies during the war I was treated at first with suspicion and even hostility. Afterwards, on reflection, I realised that all security forces are bound to adopt severe methods but at the time I blurted out " Well, gentlemen, I can only tell you that you remind me of my Russian interrogators ". My first experience of a Russian inquisition had been twelve years before.

In the summer of 1945 I had been sent for by some Russian officers in Budapest. They wanted to know why I would not cooperate with them politically, despite my interest in our liberal party, and they also asked me about my wartime activities on behalf of the British. I therefore consulted the British Military Mission in Budapest who advised me to leave the country.

I was very reluctant to do this because I was anxious to reorganise the political party in which my father had been a prominent member, and above all because my wife, who had a strong family sense, said she would not leave " the tombs of my ancestors ", as she put it. However a second interrogation, far more disagreeable than the first, convinced me that it would be wiser to cross into Austria. This I did in September.

While in Vienna I had to earn a living, so I took a temporary job at the British Headquarters; I was helped in this by a certificate from Field-Marshal Alexander in recognition of my wartime work. Yet this minor administrative job (I was little more than a clerk) was to cause me later to be shanghaied by the Russians, and to spend eight years of my life in their concentration camps.

The months went by but things did not improve in Hungary. The leaders of the Hungarian "bourgeois" parties, my father among them, were gradually being supplanted, while the Communist nominees of the Russians became more powerful. Being undecided what to do, I applied for an immigration permit to Australia, hoping that, if the situation really worsened, my wife might be prepared to start life with our children in a new continent. Vienna was too close to the tombs of her ancestors. When this permit was granted, I felt I must return to Budapest and discuss the matter with her, my father and the rest of the family. I decided that, as the Hungarian Communists would certainly not issue a visa now, I would have to enter the country illegally. Accordingly on the 4th June, 1947, I set off for the frontier with two friends who knew the crossing points.

I shall not forget that night as we crouched in the bushes near the frontier.

I had a longing to return to Vienna, a presentiment that something unpleasant would happen to me. One of my companions must have seen my fear, for he told me to pull myself together and keep an eye out for the dogs of the frontier guards.

But the crossing turned out to be uneventful (in those days there were no minefields), and twenty-four hours later, having taken the train from Györ, I found myself back in Budapest.

Before going to my wife and father in the country, I decided to call on my brother-in-law in Budapest, and consult him; for his advice was always sound. But here I received my first shock. He refused to have me in the house. He would hardly speak to me, he even seemed frightened of me. It was the same with other old friends I tried to see. "Are you mad to come back?" they said. "Don't you know what's happening here?"

At first no one would have me in their house, let alone offer me a bed; and it was not until late in the evening that, after I had telephoned several friends, all of whom made polite excuses, one of them, a doctor, saw my plight and took me in. That night in his flat was to be my last at liberty for nine years.

The next morning I was preparing to leave for the country, when the front-door bell rang. I still must have had no real apprehension of danger, for I answered it myself, (my friend had already left on his rounds). I was confronted at the door by a tall young man in civilian clothes who said, "I am a member of the security police. You must come with us for identification."

Outside on the staircase, I saw another tough-looking young man, with a revolver in his hand. I followed them downstairs. As I walked into the street the full extent of the danger struck me, and I cursed myself for having been so unimaginative. It required the actual physical appearance of the AVO men to make me appreciate my friends' warnings. Panic now possessed me, and I felt I must get away, at any cost. After walking along without exchanging a word with these men for some minutes, I acted. The first man was a little ahead of me, so I suddenly leapt at his colleague beside me and hit him hard on the jaw. He was unprepared for this and fell heavily. I turned and began running, while the other AVO man shouted to the passers-by "Catch him! He's a criminal!" He tried to grapple with me, but I managed to knock him down too. I now began running as fast as I could, but people were gathering on both sides of the street, and I soon found myself surrounded by at least fifty of them, blocking my escape on every side.

The first security man now ran up with a number of policemen who had mysteriously appeared from nowhere,

(I should have known that almost every third person in Budapest was now a policeman), and I was again arrested, this time much less ceremoniously. I was hustled into a taxi with three policemen; the AVO man uttered the words "Andrassy Ut 60," and we set off for the security police headquarters. When we arrived there I was literally kicked out of the taxi by the two men I had struck. They pulled me inside and made me stand facing the wall, my hands above my head. "Shoot him if he moves!" they said.

I had to remain like this for nearly an hour. Whenever my arms tired and I lowered them, I was given a sharp blow in the ribs with the butt of a tommy-gun. Then the security man I had knocked down came in and began punching and kicking me. At length, covered with blood, I was taken upstairs to a large room, in which behind a desk, sat an officer in civilian clothes surrounded by more policemen. To my surprise, I saw it was an old friend Istvan Timar; we had been at the university together and I had later helped him when we had both been studying law. My relief at seeing him can be imagined.

Timar glared at me. I received not a word of recognition or sympathy, not a glance of compassion.

He suddenly barked, "Why did the British send you back to Budapest?"

By now I was really frightened. "The British!" I said. "Nobody brought me back. I came on my own. From Vienna. To see my family."

"We'll see about that," he said. "Are you the son of the Liberal politician?" He knew perfectly well, of course, who my father was, but he wanted to pretend he had never had anything to do with me.

"Yes, I am," I said, adding that my father was now

an old man, and that he had no intention of returning to politics.

"Why did you," continued this friend, "who once showed proper democratic tendencies, leave us? And not only did you leave us, but you went to Vienna to work for our enemies."

"Haven't you heard of my work for the British during the war?" I asked. "Helping their escaped prisoners to get away from the Nazis? I did the same for the Jews. And for the Dutch. And for many Hungarians."

"That's true," he said. "You may have helped the Jews against Fascism once, we know that. But what have you been doing since? You've changed sides." He then began shouting again. "What were your contacts with the British in Vienna? Why did you go there? What was your job? You're a spy! Who gave you orders to organise spying in Hungary?"

I repeated that I had no idea what he was talking about, that I had never had the slightest connection with espionage, and that my job at the British Military Mission had been a minor one.

"Well, we'll try something else then," he said. "Take this piece of paper, sit at that table, and write down the whole story of the time you spent with the British in Vienna. If you do that fully and frankly, you may be able to save your skin."

He left me with the paper and pen for what must have been nearly two hours, and I wrote as accurately as I could about my activities in Vienna with the British. When he returned, he looked through the three or four pages scornfully. "Take him out!" he said to the guards. "We'll give him twenty-four hours to think it over. Then perhaps he'll talk."

I was taken into another room without windows, and which was lit by an extremely strong lamp. Here they made me stand against a wall while they went through my pockets. I was roughly undressed, receiving a number of blows on the head and in the stomach, one of which caused me such a sharp jabbing pain in the kidneys that I collapsed. I was then forced to hold my feet upwards so that they could beat the soles. Then the upper part of my feet and my ankles were beaten, until they were swollen and bleeding.

I spent the night in this cell—my only consolation being a loaf of bread and a blanket sent by my sister—and the following day I was taken back for further interrogation. My ex-lawyer friend had now been replaced by a senior officer whom everyone addressed as "colonel." (I learnt later that before 1945, this "colonel" had been a muncipal fireman.) "We know that you belong to the British espionage service," he said. "Only by admitting the truth have you any chance of saving your life."

He questioned me about certain British and American organisations in Austria. I could, of course, give no proper answers to any of these questions, because I knew nothing about them. I had never heard of them.

"All right," he said, at length. "You're stubborn I see. If you won't talk to us, perhaps you'd prefer to talk to the Russians. They'll be interested in you. You're a fool not to tell us the truth. You'll see what happens now. What you've just had is paradise compared with what you're in for."

2

Russian Interrogation

JULY 1947

The Russian major who now interrogated me had the high cheekbones and slanting eyes of a Mongolian, and I had a feeling of having been handed over to Asiatics. Through an interpreter, he repeated the accusation that I had deserted to the greatest of their enemies, the British.

He then surprised me by mentioning the name of a British airman, whom I had helped escape from Hungary during the war, Reginald Barratt. In December 1944 I had helped Barratt cross to the Russian lines with special information which we had received by secret radio from the Western Allies. My interrogator made the sinister observation that Reginald Barratt had really been a member of the British Intelligence Service, and had been caught working in Russia as a double agent. He was now dead.*

He then went on and mentioned another old friend of mine, a Budapest dentist called Miklos Csomos who had also worked in the underground movement during the war and knew Barratt. He said Csomos was now serving a life sentence in Russia for his hostility to the Russians.

*In fact, Barratt was not a double agent; he was nevertheless shot in Russia on 4th June, 1945. His name is inscribed on the R.A.F. War Memorial at Runnymede.

"Do you want to end up the same way?" the major asked. "We believe you are one of the most dangerous members of the British military intelligence."

As the interrogation continued, he mentioned the names of further British and American officers and civilians working for the Allied headquarters in Vienna. He appeared to have the most detailed knowledge and was clearly anxious to impress me with the efficiency of the Russian security system. Having failed to obtain a "confession" he said irritably, "I must agree with your countrymen. You're very stubborn. But as your life depends on it, we'll give you plenty of time to think things over."

This was the first of a number of interrogations by this Mongolian officer, in the course of which he mentioned the names of many of my Austrian friends, even of my relations who lived in Vienna. He referred to telephone calls I had made in Vienna, and told me their subject. He read out conversations I had had with these friends. Almost verbatim! I was astounded by his knowledge.

"We have time," he said at length. "We know all about you. We can afford to wait until you feel inclined to talk."

"If you know everything about me, then why go on interrogating me?" I said. "Why keep me in this prison?"

One day during an interrogation, he made an offer which I half-expected. Seeing that he still could not obtain the "confession" he wanted, he suggested that I should work for the Russians, because my connections with the Western allies would make me very suitable for espionage work! I refused of course; and the next day (it was early August 1947) I was taken by car, handcuffed, to the Russian military headquarters in Baden, near Vienna.

It seems strange that this quiet watering place, Baden, in its green setting of fields and woods near Vienna, with its memories of elderly valetudinarians in wheel-chairs, of Franz-Joseph and his court, a typically Habsburg spa, should be the scene of my grimmest interrogation. But the Soviet High Command had chosen it as the H.Q. for their armies in Central Europe. It was now almost a Russian town.

I was interrogated nightly, but in a much more leisurely, if a more thorough way, as if eternity lay before us. I must have repeated myself a hundred times in the next eight months. The Russians knew no Hungarian, and I no Russian, so the proceedings were conducted in German, which did not facilitate matters. Minutes were taken slowly, and for every question, which I answered shortly, the interpreter would write for as long as an hour. The Russians, I discovered, are masters in the art of breaking down the morale of the prisoner. After what the Hungarian colonel had told me, I had imagined that they would torture me, physically. But their method was to impose everlasting interrogations, and dreary prison conditions, which induce at length a feeling of utter hopelessness and despair.

As soon as I fell asleep at night in my cell, I would be shaken by guards and dragged upstairs to face the endless drumfire of the same old questions. Plain-clothes and uniformed officers would come in and whisper seriously to my interrogators, as if bringing special orders from higher quarters. They would look at me quizzically, as if I was some *rara avis*, and would sometimes ask me questions too. Then, looking very wise, they would make copious notes.

Bright reflectors were sometimes turned on to my face, and four or five interrogators would appear mysteriously and place themselves in corners of the room, where I could not see them. Then I would be attacked from all sides, the same questions repeated as many as fifteen times a night. Dead tired, I would be taken back to my damp cell—until it all started again the next night.

My interrogators were interested in everything and everybody I knew, down to the most remote school acquaintances whom I had not met for years. The manner in which they inquired about these friends was most ingenious. They knew that I was worried about my family, my friends and relations, and was frightened of involving them in trouble. They knew that *I knew* that anyone who had had anything to do with me, a "British spy," might now be in danger. They therefore told me to speak of these friends quite openly, claiming that, anyhow, they knew all about them already. Often the interrogator would mention a name casually, in passing from one subject to another, to watch my reactions. He would say they were simply trying to see if I were "decent," whether I told the truth or not.

The small hints about one's possible "decency"—a kind of promise that they did not really want to harm one—gives the prisoner in solitary confinement a feeling that the interrogators are not necessarily his enemies. As they questioned me they smiled, that eternal smile, the Communist smile, calm, cynical, official. How well I was to get to know it in the next eight years!

"Old so-and-so, you haven't seen him for ten years, you say. Then," looking at me knowingly, "why did you draw him into your spy circle as a British agent?" I professed blank amazement, but they continued imperturbably. What were his tasks? When had he entered the British service? Why did *he*, of all decent

Hungarians, act against the progressive democratic countries?

Weeks passed, months passed in solitary confinement. Sometimes I was told that I would be confronted with a certain person I knew—to-morrow, the day after, next week—Rosen, Bauer, Csomos, other officials I had known or heard of at the British H.Q. in Vienna. But the men with these names never came.

A less pleasant way of trying to persuade the prisoner to talk is to describe his future if he is "unco-operative." The lead and copper mines in Siberia, the coal mines in the Arctic tundra were described to me in loving detail. One of the interrogators spoke of life in the eternal snows and the gold mines of Kolyma in the Far East; of the hopelessness in the lumber camps thousands of miles from civilisation; of the exhausting labour on the new railway lines stretching out across the vast continent; of the lethal canal building. Lastly, he described the concentration camps where the prisoners lived.

They told me there was no hope of escape from these camps. Their inhabitants would still be human beings in fifteen or twenty years' time, still alive to feel pain and hardship. How stupid the Germans had been to kill their prisoners! The Gestapo had foolishly tortured them so that they sometimes died! "Ridiculous!" my interrogator said. "We make our prisoners work. Why kill them? They can work until the last minute of their lives —all for us. When they cannot work any more, *then* they can die."

Such was life in Baden. It was worse for me than for the other prisoners, because I was not allowed out for exercise; I did not know when the sun was shining or the stars were out. As a British spy I was completely isolated.

In these months of loneliness I searched for any sign,

any trace of life, which might keep me in contact with the world outside. I obtained a strange satisfaction from watching the spiders in the corner of their webs. I watched the flies come in through the iron grille, and thought, "How lucky they are! They're free! But how foolish to come in here of all places!"

I watched the spider contemplating his prey in his independent little universe; the interminable fight of the fly for life, the victory of the strong over the weak. I saw the flies moving into the web and the astute spider first numbing them with his sting, then ripping up the unsuspecting wanderer who had come from the free world in search of something—to find only death. Was there not some resemblance between my predicament and that of the fly?

Later, I discovered in one of the corners of the cell an old chimney hatch that had been plastered over. The plaster was cracked and in one of the cracks I became aware of life; an animal was trying to get out. I watched for days, hoping this time not for insect, but for animal company. At last, my patience was rewarded. One day, a tiny pointed nose appeared in the crack; then I saw two sparkling little black eyes, and two erect ears. A mouse came out and stared curiously around the cellar, as if looking for something. It approached me, even glanced up at me. Then it sat up on its two hind legs! A few morsels of prisoners' bread were on the floor and the mouse ran over to them, at the same time watching me carefully. I did not move, and tried to convey to it, "But, my friend, there's nothing to fear from me. We are both prisoners here."

In the next few weeks I discovered a whole new world. My companion had a family, and one day she brought in even smaller mice. If I kept very still, they would play in front of me. They came to know me well, they would eat the morsels of bread I gave them, almost out of my hand.

In spite of this companionship I later fell into a coma, a state of semi-consciousness which lasted for about ten days. During this I was not taken for interrogations, and I remember being given injections by the prison doctor. I must have sat for nearly a week without moving in one of the damp corners of the cell, where feverish dreams and hallucinations visited me. I saw, or thought I saw, shadows, moving silhouettes on the wall taking on human forms. I saw the head of Christ; then the head and shoulders of a Franciscan monk who held a Cross out in his hands towards me. I saw what seemed to be an angel, fluttering down in the clouds towards me, its long robes flowing out behind.

If these visions bewildered me, they also gave me hope of salvation.

On the 23rd April, 1948, eight months after my arrival in Baden (I had by then, completely lost all count of time), I was tried by a Russian court martial. I was taken upstairs into a large room in which, behind a table covered with a red cloth, sat three Russian officers. The president of the court charged me with high treason and espionage against Hungary and the Soviet Union.

Between the pages of the extensive minutes of my interrogation, slips of paper had been placed as markers, and as he turned the pages he put a series of sharp questions. He did not read the entire minutes; that would have taken weeks. Instead, he asked if I understood the selected paragraphs. I was amazed at the lies and falsifications they contained. Sometimes I recognised a name, but most of the statements attributed to me I had never uttered. I asked how all this nonsense had got into the minutes. With an ironical smile, he said, "This is your confession. In your own words."

It was now my turn to smile. "You appear to be taking these statements for granted," I said. "You are evidently already convinced of my guilt. There seems little point in my attempting to defend myself."

I had heard before about the infamous "telegram tribunals" in which the prisoner is sentenced by telegram from Moscow, the *troika* method as it is called; I suspected that this was what had happened. I was sure that the telegram sentencing me lay there on the table beside the minutes. All these formalities and minute readings were a farce. I said that I had no means of calling witnesses; there was no counsel for my defence, although, according to Russian law, this was obligatory. "So, gentlemen," I said, "I'm completely in your hands. You can do what you like with me. There seems little point in attempting to present my case. You evidently know my sentence already. You are my prosecutors, not my judges."

The president replied that I knew how to argue. "That is as it should be," he said. "You are a lawyer. But that makes your crime worse. As an educated man, you should have used your knowledge in support of democracy."

The whole procedure of reading from the selected minutes lasted about an hour. Then, to my amazement, I heard what seemed like words of comfort. "Do not be afraid," he said. "If you work well after your sentence in the punishment camp, and show a respectful attitude, it may be possible to grant clemency later. You may be freed within the borders of the Soviet Union. There you will be able to work as an equal with everyone else. You will be able to join in the noble work of building socialism. You will see what a more humane life you will have in the new society. After a while, you will realise that you are disillusioned with the capitalist world."

I was then sentenced to twenty-five years' forced labour.*

Neunkirchen, my first destination on the long journey to Russia, is on the Austro-Hungarian border; and here I was taken the next day, with a number of other convicted prisoners. Our hands were bound, for Baden is not far from the British and American zones, and many prisoners must have contemplated escape. I could hardly stand on my feet, so dizzy was I when I saw the light of day again.

It is hard to describe what a strange feeling it is, after eight months in a dark cell, to come out into the open. My first impression was of the colour—of its vividness and variety, the *green* greenness of the fields, the *blue* blueness of the sky, the dazzling white of the whitewashed cottages. These colours struck me in the eye, as if my retina had taken on another sensitivity, like that in the vision of a deep water fish, attuned to the subtlest gradations of grey and black. I even felt, in that first half hour, while waiting for the prison van, a strange longing to be back in my grey world with the mice and the spiders, to return to the womb of the cell.

The transit prison in Neunkirchen had once been a Nazi "model prison." Hitler had operated here three years before; now Stalin had taken over from him. It was surrounded by high brick walls, with barbed wire on the top, and in each corner of the courtyard were wooden towers with guards looking down on us, armed

*In any other year I would have received the death penalty, but for reasons explained in the appendix I escaped this.

with tommy-guns. Here, in this modern building where no expense had been spared, for there were even fine beds of geraniums in the centre, was twentieth-century civilisation indeed!

It was here for the first time since my arrest, nearly a year before, that I found human company again. Some of the prisoners had undergone similar confinements, and our first words as the key turned in our new cell behind us were happy ones. The first phase of our torment was over, and we discussed, almost with clinical curiosity, our unpredictable future. Most of my new companions had by now acquired a kind of happy-go-lucky lightheartedness, an indifference almost to the free world outside the prison walls.

All convicted prisoners were sent to Neunkirchen before setting out for Russia, and we had a varied assortment of nationalities in our cell. It was soon filled until we numbered thirty-five, all dragged up in the vast shrimping net which the Russians had cast into Central and Eastern Europe: Czechs, Slovaks, British, Rumanians, Hungarians, Americans, Austrians, Yugoslavs, Germans, even Russians, jostled one another, slept cheek by jowl. Each had his story to tell, each described his capture, and spoke indignantly of his alleged crime. Every day for weeks, groups of these assorted peoples would be assembled in what was known as an *étappe*, or travelling group, and sent off in cattle or prisoner trucks for their distant goal, the work camps of Russia.

Among this congeries of nations I soon heard of tragedies other than my own, and I became accustomed to condoling with other prisoners over their fate. A new critical sense, a new awareness possessed me, and I realised that I could never have learned so much about human life in the free world outside. Here, in this inferno of suffering, I heard of ordeals beside which my own seemed small; and I even reached a state of peace of mind. I was aware that a great new human migration was going on around me, and that in this ferment, this twentieth-century avalanche, I was only a tiny piece of gravel.

3

Prisons on Wheels

Each of the *étappes* I have described contained prisoners, guilty, broadly speaking, of one particular "crime." I and a number of others were in the worst category, as "British and American spies," and it took some months before there were enough of us to be worth moving. We had to wait from May until December, when our cells had become so crowded that we were sleeping on top of one another.

One wintry morning we were ordered to change into old Russian uniforms. The hands and feet of the "most dangerous" (myself included) were bound with wire, and we were thrown like so many sacks of potatoes into waiting lorries. Some six hundred of us were then taken in a convoy to Neunkirchen railway station, where we found a special prisoners' train waiting for us. It consisted of about fifty wagons, each equipped with bunks for thirty-five prisoners, and staffed with three guards. These guards lived on the trains, shuttling back and forth across Russia, always accompanying prisoners. After years of this, they had lost all human feeling; one could read the callousness and brutality on their faces. They told us that any attempt at escape would mean instant death, and when we reached the Hungarian frontier, one of them said to me, "We're now travelling

41

through Hungary. You're a Hungarian, so don't give any trouble or shout to your people. It'll be a quick death, if you do." I had hoped that the wire would be taken off my hands and feet, but it was removed only from my legs. Fortunately, another prisoner, a friendly Austrian eased it on my wrists a little.

While we crossed Hungary, even the guards were confined in their compartments, so that all communication with the locals might be prevented. When we reached Budapest they took even greater precautions. We were made to lie in our bunks and remain motionless for hours, until the train left. On the way, I heard Hungarian voices, of the railwaymen, tapping the wheels beneath our wagon. Yet I could not tell them that I was bound for slavery in Russia.

Conditions were appalling. There was no water and, for a W.C., we used a hole at the end of the wagon. Often, during the long journey in the central European winter, older prisoners missed the hole, and the wagon soon overflowed with filth. One of the most embarrassing features was that in some of the opposite bunks were women. Even more embarrassing—those of us whose hands were tied had to be assisted at the W.C. But we were so exhausted, that we soon became indifferent to sex distinctions.

Our food, which was produced in a kitchen wagon at the end of the train, consisted of watery cabbage soup, with two or three leaves, sometimes maize soup, occasionally, cold fish. Some of the older prisoners were soon in agony, caused by eating this salt fish and having nothing to drink. Those whose hands were tied had to be fed by the others.

It was mid-winter, but the wagons had no stoves or any form of heating, and we were wearing old, threadbare Russian uniforms. Some Russian prisoners evolved an ingenious way of making a fire. They undid the seams of their caps and jackets and extracted small bits of cotton wool and fluff which had collected there, which they twisted into compact masses. They then took off their boots, and ground the cotton-wool so violently on the floor beneath their soles that it produced friction and caught alight. Some of the prisoners had twigs or small pieces of wood, with which they could, for a short time, warm their hands.

On this four-day journey, five prisoners died, including a young Ukrainian with whom I had made friends in Neunkirchen. He had been dead a day when we reached the Russian frontier, but the guards left his corpse in the wagon with the other prisoners. "It's a cold winter," one of them said. "He won't stink for a day or two."

At the Russian frontier, the railway gauge changed, and we were transferred to Russian wagons, cattle trucks whose windows were sealed with iron plates. We also had a fresh set of guards, who checked everything again. They were particularly interested in our personal belongings, and I realised that toothbrushes, cigarette holders and socks were evidently luxuries in Russia. They stole these, and we heard them arguing as to who should possess them.

The journey to our first destination in Russia, Lvov, took two days. Lvov is only a hundred and seventy miles inside Russia, but the area was still full of Ukrainian partisans, and large-scale skirmishes with them were continually taking place in the mountains and valleys. The authorities were careful therefore not to allow prisoners' trains to run at night through the mountain passes and lonely forests of the Carpathians, where they could easily be attacked by the Ukrainian partisans. Some prisoners said that supplies of food and ammunition were regularly parachuted to these partisans from the West.

Our Ukrainian fellow-prisoners told us that orders were sent from partisan headquarters to smaller groups; they explained how reports and news were distributed; how Russian trains were derailed, depots and *kolkhozes** attacked; how the local inhabitants were compelled to give the partisans food, lodging, information. Had they not done this, they said, they would have been attacked by the partisans as traitors. Some of the Ukrainian prisoners in our wagon had been sentenced by the Russians for giving shelter, if for only a few hours, to a partisan, or for having offered him food. For such a crime, fifteen to twenty years sentence was not uncommon.

The Ukrainian partisans often attacked prison trains at night and liberated their inmates. This was why our train stood the whole night in the stations with other engines, all blowing their whistles, as if, by so doing, they might help one another's morale.

The Russian wagons had stoves, but the few logs of wood which were now thrown in at night, burned in an hour or so. As we crossed the Carpathians the cold became more intense, and when we arrived at Lvov, the prisoners who had caught pneumonia, and were still alive, were bundled together into separate lorries and taken to the prison hospital.

We all had great hopes of Lvov. The skilful propaganda of the Russian political officers in Neunkirchen may have been responsible for this, for the news had spread that the inhuman prison conditions we had lived under during the interrogations would cease when we reached the Soviet Union. Most of us believed that a comparatively

*Collective farms.

better future, even if it meant hard work, awaited us. The Russian prisoners also spoke of better conditions, saying that we would be taken to the industrial centres of the Ukraine.

But our treatment in the Lvov transit camp was, if anything, worse than it had been in Austria. When we arrived at the station, a group of yelling MVD* officials bundled us into large black vans, twenty-five or thirty squeezed into a space for twelve. Arms and legs hung out at the end, but the guards simply banged the doors on them. I was at the bottom of a pile of prisoners, hardly able to breathe.

The most memorable feature of the Lvov transit camp was my first acquaintance with the "bandits," a ruthless organisation which flourished inside, and outside, the prisons of Russia, a kind of Klu Klux Klan terrorising other prisoners throughout the territories of the entire Soviet Union. In some ways, these men were more powerful than the guards.

Our Ukrainian friends had already spoken of the murders and robberies the bandits committed in the camps, and I had been only a week in Lvov when I realised that these men were now among us. I learned to recognise them by the way they congregated together, and attacked fellow prisoners, generally for their food or clothes. When any of us protested, they warned us to keep quiet; if we did not, they said, they would kill us.

"Just you fit in," one of them said to me "or you'll be for trouble. You Europeans have had a better time than we've ever had. We've never had anything. Leave us to get what we want the way we want!"

It took me months to understand the psychology of these sinister men, perhaps a hundred thousand of them spread out over the entire penal network of Russia, who

*MVD—the Russian Security Police.

were a law unto themselves; and to realise that the prison authorities were unable to do anything about it.*

One morning, an old Ukrainian peasant complained that a food parcel he had received from his relations had been stolen during the night. We knew what had happened, because some of the bandits had been eyeing his food the night before. They had withdrawn into a corner of the cell, as was their habit, and talked quietly among themselves.

A courageous young Ukrainian who saw that the old man could not defend himself, accused the bandits of this theft. "We've had enough of you brutes," he said. "We won't have any more stealing in this cell. You're a minority among us. You've been doing what you like until now. Now you're going to give him back his parcel."

The rest of us were so encouraged by this that when the bandits attacked him, we came to his rescue. We tore up the planks from the bunks, and lashed out at the bandits, who retaliated. Soon blood began to flow. I received a blow on the head from a young Ukrainian which almost knocked me out. (He later told me I was so filthy and unrecognisable that he had mistaken me for a bandit!) Some of the Ukrainians threw heavy earthenware mugs at the bandits, one of whom received a broken mug in the face. Another collapsed with a huge gash in his neck. After a quarter of an hour of pandemonium, the door burst open, and guards armed with steel rods strode in. They immediately began lashing about in every direction, and I received another blow which I felt for weeks afterwards. When it was all over, two prisoners were carried off unconscious, a Ukrainian

*Had I then read Dostoievsky's stories from *The House of the Dead*, I would have known that these bandits are indigenous to Russia; they existed in Tsarist times too.

had his ear torn off, and another man's nose and arm were broken.

The authorities conducted an inquiry the next day, examining us individually. Our Ukrainian friends warned us not to incriminate the bandits, because we could never be sure when we might meet them again. The bandits' bush telegraph between the various camps was very effective, as I was to discover later. "People have been murdered," the Ukrainian told us, "when they arrive in a new prison for denouncing a bandit in another prison thousands of miles away."

We therefore told the prison authorities that a quarrel had started, in the heat of which two groups had formed, both equally to blame. The interrogating officer knew perfectly well what had happened, of course, but he smiled, and no one was punished. Such then was my introduction to the prisons of Russia. In ordinary gaols, the prisoner's worst enemy is the gaoler. Here we found a more insidious enemy—among our fellow sufferers.

In the new year, before the journey to Central Russia, I was medically examined. The doctors were women (wearing MVD officers' uniforms) one of whom became interested in my personal possessions. Our Russian gaolers were often prepared to give us food in exchange for some personal belonging which we had brought from the West; and this female coveted the wool blanket my sister had sent me when I was arrested. She told one of my cell companions that if he could persuade me to hand it over, she would prescribe extra food for him. This man, Zoltan Varga, was in a very poor state of health. I knew he needed more food before the long journey to Central Russia, so I gave it to him. For this he acquired from the doctor half a pound of margarine, a spoonful of millet, and about two ounces of bread a day. I soon learned that there was really little point in keeping possessions of this kind, because they would sooner or later be stolen anyway by the bandits.

The day before we left for Central Russia, I saw some girls, all of whom must have been under fourteen, exercising in the prison yard; and I was told that they had been sentenced for distributing "Ukrainian nationalist propaganda." That children should be treated as criminals, in the same prison as the bandits, seemed to me the depths of barbarity! One day I saw a prisoner hanging from a barbed-wire fence with his stomach ripped wide open by the wire—and these little girls passing beside him on their way to exercise.

It was not until March 1949 that special officials came to select us according to our physique and working capacity. We stood in front of them naked, and the prison doctors informed them about us. One prisoner they thought might be fit for the Arctic or the forests of the Far East; another, better suited for the Volga district; another, for the marshes where the new canals were being built, the coal mines of Vorkuta in the tundra, or perhaps the Central Asian metal mines. When my turn came, I was allotted to "Labour Camp 10." I had no idea what this meant, or where it was.

We left Lvov one morning early in March, 1949, in the depths of a Russian winter. In spite of this, some of us still thought of escaping. Little did we know what the word "escape" means in these endless plains in the winter.

The prison wagons were larger than those used in Europe. They had come from the camps in Central Russia to collect us, and were specially equipped for prisoners. They were much wider, with three separate tiers of bunks, two along the sides and one in the centre of the compartment. There was an iron stove, and a primitive W.C. at the end of the wagon. The train was also equipped with a kitchen wagon, but during the first days we were given no hot food, only salted fish and a pound or so of black prisoners' bread. By some oversight, there was no water. It may seem strange that anyone surrounded by such expanses of snow should feel the torments of thirst; but we greedily scratched down the hoar frost from the inside walls of the wagon, and sucked it.

There were about eighty prisoners in our wagon, and a struggle immediately took place for bunks. Everyone wanted to have the top bunk, which was warmer. The older prisoners and the Europeans like ourselves proved to be less skilled in this struggle, and we soon found ourselves at the bottom.

The method of guarding the train was still very elaborate. Between the wagons, special platforms for guards and machine-gun emplacements had been constructed, with powerful searchlights placed on the top. In each wagon were guards, some of whom had dogs. And there was telephonic communication between them and the commander's car. Our Ukrainian friends proudly told us that these precautions were necessary as long as we were in the Ukraine, among their partisans.

The first night we really believed that these Ukrainian partisans *had* attacked. The brakes were suddenly applied and the train stopped convulsively. We heard feverish shouts, the barking of dogs, and orders yelled hoarsely from one end of the train to the other. The door of our wagon was thrown open, and MVD guards rushed in, ordering us to leave our bunks and assemble in one corner. Prisoners slow to obey received a sharp blow from the big wooden hammers they carried. They then carefully examined the bunks and floorboards. We hoped that the partisans had made a raid. But it was only a test, to see if we had made holes in the wall, or tried to loosen the boards.

Like some armoured convoy, our slave train moved on through the famous forests of Briansk. Everywhere, on all sides, was forest, stretching from Galicia and the Carpathians to Moscow, nearly fifteen hundred miles ahead. It was only now that I understood what distance means in Russia, and a new despondency, a feeling of utter hopelessness, came over me.

At first we passed towns and villages which bore some resemblance to those in Europe. But they soon degenerated into groups of tumble-down little cottages, agglomerations of hovels, whose inhabitants, in rags and tatters, revealed that conditions were worse here than in Poland or the Ukraine. And as for my native countryside, with its wooded hills and valleys and the fertile plains, (the *puszta*), it seemed a Canaan to this.

The older prisoners suffered most during the twelve-day journey; in the intense cold they could not control their bodies, and the smell in the wagon soon became unbearable. One of them whom I remember especially was a Ukrainian who had been sentenced for helping the partisans. He told me that he had unwisely returned from America in the thirties (he had emigrated there and made a small fortune), and bought a farm in Galicia. He survived the German occupation, but when the Ukrainian partisans asked for food and shelter he gladly gave it. "Anyway," he said, "if I had not given it, they would have taken it. I am an old man, my wife is dead, and my daughters were not in the house. I was alone. What could I do? I'm over seventy-four. What have I to expect now from life? I am ready to die. May the Good Lord take me!"

Two days later I found him lying beside me in the early morning, motionless, his eyes wide open, staring;

his body was stiff, and he had evidently been dead for some hours.

We had to travel on with his body for several days, and when we arrived at our destination I learned that there were several other corpses on the train.

By now I was beginning to lose control of my body too, passing water in my sleep, waking to find my trousers frozen to the floor. At first, I tried to conceal this, but when I realised it was happening to everyone, I discussed it with the others, although there was little we could do to help one another.

On the seventh day we reached Moscow, where we spent forty-eight hours while the wagon was shunted about in various goods yards on the outskirts, and some pompous officials came to examine us. They went from wagon to wagon, smiling sardonically, counting us as if we were sheep.

After Moscow, the scenery changed; the endless forests gave way to equally endless and featureless plains, across which we travelled for three days. During the last two days we were given no food, and the Ukrainians said that the guards were selling our miserable rations to the civilian population at the stations we passed through. So bad was the local food that the people would gladly pay for our dry salted fish, the ground oats and maize. Our frozen military bread also found customers.

Towards the end of the third day, the railway line ran out into a land of low bushes and marshes, and someone cried from a bunk above, "The camps are ahead! The camps are ahead!"

We all became immensely excited, anxious to see these notorious camps where we might have to spend the rest of our lives.

II. RUSSIA

1949-1954

4

Quarantine

MARCH 1949

We looked out through the grilles, and saw a maze of wooden palisades, hutments, watch-towers, miles of barbed wire, and groups of prisoners in torn, quilted clothes accompanied by guards and dogs. As the train moved slowly on, we passed at least ten of these camps. We were in a new environment, a kind of national park, a human zoo.

The perimeter of Camp 10 consisted of a palisade about twenty feet high surrounded by barbed wire, which projected inwards and outwards. There was a second barbed-wire fence outside this, in which were a number of watch-towers, about a hundred yards apart. On each of these hung a five foot iron rail, which the guards would hit from time to time to inform the neighbouring towers that they were on the alert. The corner towers were equipped with machine-guns and searchlights.

At the gates I saw for the first time another curious gadget of camp life with which I was to become familiar, a piece of birch wood shaped like a slate. The guards used this when counting prisoners at roll calls. They scratched a figure on it, which they would erase later with a piece of broken glass—an interesting comment on the shortage of paper in the Soviet Union. The only writing materials in the camp were bits of birch and sharp

55

instruments, pieces of flint or glass which served as pencils.

The inmates of the camp, mostly old and crippled prisoners, were loitering about staring at us, but they were sharply ordered back into their huts. Some of us had become so weak during the journey that they had to be carried on stretchers by their friends. We were taken into a large barracks which had been divided off from the rest of the camp by a barbed-wire fence, the quarantine barracks for new prisoners.

While waiting, some of my companions went up to the barbed-wire fence to look round, but the guards in the watch-towers waved them away. One prisoner did not move quickly enough, and the guards shot in the air behind him. I was to discover that the guards in this camp were very quick on the trigger; if they disliked a prisoner they would shoot near him. When the administrative arrangements had been completed, the checking of names, numbers, ages, etc., we were divided into groups and taken to the baths.

The temperature outside was thirty degrees below centigrade zero, and even in the bathroom it was below freezing point. We had to strip completely and were then admitted to the bath, a big wooden tub nine feet high, twelve feet in diameter, where we were given two pails of water and a small piece of brown soap. Meanwhile, our clothes were taken away by elderly prisoners for *schmom* (searching of pockets), and disinfecting.

It was so cold that we all washed quickly, only to find that we had to wait naked and shivering for half an hour until the clothes were brought back. While we were dressing, one of the elderly prisoners who had been in charge of the clothes, seemed anxious to talk to me. He spoke German, and said how sorry he was to see a young man like myself in such a place. "Do you know what kind of camp this is?" he asked.

I said I imagined it was like any other Russian concentration camp. I supposed they were all much the same.

"No," he said. "You are in the camp for the worst political offenders. Old Tsarist officers like myself, dangerous spies, high Communist officials who have fallen into disgrace, Leninists, Trotskyists, scientists who have offended authority. That is why this camp is nearer Moscow than the others. Not in Siberia. They want to keep an eye on you." He looked at me intently, and then said, "No one has ever left this camp alive."

He told me he was an ex-staff officer, who had fought the Reds during the revolution. He was captured and imprisoned, but released in the twenties. Later, in Stalin's time, he was imprisoned again, and sent to this camp. All his relations were dead, so he had no wish to leave it. He doubted if he could ever find his place again in the modern world. No one would now understand him; he was only waiting for God to relieve him of his sufferings.

"All the same," he said, "I can't bear to see young chaps like you in this camp. You still have something to live for. We are all suffering for a better, Christian way of life. All we can do is to accept the suffering God imposes. You, my boy, must regard your fate as a good Christian should. Suffer it with dignity and patience." He was so touched by his own words that he started to cry.

I told him it was not enough to accept suffering passively; I agreed that we must keep our faith in God, and said that I knew He would not allow such injustice to go on indefinitely. "I know," I said, "that we shall live to see better days. In a free and happier world. We shall enjoy life again."

This conversation made a deep impression on me. Although it depressed me, it was a help in the first hours of my life in the camps, to meet such a man. His religious conviction strengthened the determination, which I had developed since my arrest, that the only way in which I could stand suffering would be by putting myself into the hands of God.

All new prisoners had to pass through the quarantine period, partly to undergo a medical inspection which would allot us to our work; partly, I believe, to prevent our talking with the other prisoners, and spreading optimistic stories about the West. After a month or six weeks, any information the newcomer brings is out of date, and (this was psychologically most ingenious) our enthusiasm and desire to spread news had diminished.

As the period of quarantine passed in idleness, and we had no more personal stories to tell one another, a mood of general depression replaced the first optimism. Some of us were more cold than hungry; others more hungry than cold. The food was execrable—thin cabbage soup, mush from half hulled grain, and a pound of bread, a heavy black dough, containing fifty per cent water. Our ration was small because this was an invalid camp, for the weaker prisoners in the low working categories. This resulted in continuous bartering. Those who had managed to bring a scarf, a vest, or piece of warm clothing, would exchange it for a few pieces of dry bread. I exchanged some of my clothes for bread in this way, but I regretted it. For a few hours' relief from hunger, I lost a warm pullover.

There was no heating, but one advantage of being overcrowded (we slept almost on top of one another) was that we generated warmth on our own. Bloodstains from previous battles with bed-bugs were visible on all the bunks, and we were soon fighting the losing battle with this vermin.

We used snow for bath water. For tooth-brushes, we used our fingers, and soap for paste.

A guard had been placed at the entrance of the quarantine block to prevent us talking with other prisoners. He was not armed—a safety precaution I learned, because prisoners in the past had often attacked guards and stolen their weapons. But sometimes, if he was not looking, we could approach the wire fence in the quarantine barracks, and exchange a few words with the old men who were clearing away the snow. It was often so high around the palisades that even the top of the fence was covered. This made escape easier in the winter, and explained why the older men, incapable of anything else, were regularly sent out to clear it as it fell. Most of them had Mongolian or Chinese faces (some were Turkmen or Kazakstakian) and I had great difficulty in telling the difference between the various eastern faces I saw across the palisades.

After two weeks the snow fell so heavily that even the quarantine prisoners were used to clear it near the railway lines. We still wore our tattered old Russian uniforms, which were poor protection in this climate, and I had a greatcoat which was tied together with bits of string. Our clothes were often fastened in this way because, when we were searched, which was fairly often, the *schmom* was conducted in such a brusque manner that the buttons were torn off. Later, we were given caps, padded with cotton wool, and old military boots.

As the days of waiting in quarantine passed, some of the more daring prisoners who had been years in the camp, sneaked into our barracks to talk and find out all about us. One of these was a Hungarian cobbler, a Communist, who had fled to Russia in a fit of idealism. I liked him, but my friends warned me that he might be an informer who had been sent in to find out what we talked about.

My greatest surprise (and delight) was to meet Miklos Csomos, who had worked in the same underground movement in the war. I have mentioned that, during my interrogation in Baden, the Russians had threatened me with the "same fate as Csomos's." Sure enough, here we were in the same camp! But when we met we did not at first recognise one another. He had been a huge bear-like fellow, and I remembered him radiating good health and energy. The man who approached me now had hollow cheeks; the great frame seemed shrunken and emaciated. The ghost of the man I had known came towards me. Only his irrepressible good humour and love of life remained. He roared with laughter when he recognised me, and slapped me on the back.

"Raphael!" he cried. "You look as if you had gone through a mangle. What have they done to you?"

"What have they done to *you*?" I said. "You must have lost five stone."

"Yes," he said philosophically. "The food here is not exactly nourishing. Not like those meals we used to eat together on the Margaret Island. But it's marvellous to see you again, you old rogue! What did they get you for?"

I told him my story, and talked about our work for the western allies and the political views he had shared with me and my father. "Yes, yes," he said. "The mad son of a mad father! We all stood up to the Germans. Now we are standing up to the Russians. And here we are! This is what Liberal politics have done to us!"

He had been sentenced to death in Hungary by the

Communists, and had remained forty days in the death cell. For forty days and nights he never knew if, when the cell door opened, he was to be taken out into the yard and, like many whose cries he had heard, hanged. His sentence had finally been commuted, and here he was serving a term of twenty-five years' hard labour.

He had arrived some years before me, and the camp administration had soon discovered his dental qualifications. They now used him as their family doctor. He had a privileged position, working in the hospital block, which enabled him to obtain drugs for the weaker prisoners from the special police stock, and permits for the sick, exempting them from work. In the days to come Miklos did everything he could to help us. When the end of the quarantine period was approaching, a Russian general, Sergienko, visited our barracks and made a short speech, asking if we had any complaints. Two Lithuanian boys came forward, claiming that they should not be punished as the adults; they asked to be transferred to a youth camp. They said they had been too young to know what they were doing, and they courageously expressed their dislike of Communism. The older prisoners who understood this (the Lithuanians spoke Russian, because Lithuania had been under Soviet rule for some years, and they had learnt Russian in school) held their breath, fearing that the Russian general would lose his temper, and punishments would follow for everyone. But the general showed no emotion.

"You are old enough to know you committed a crime," he said. "You are, in fact, doubly guilty, because you received a good education in Lithuania. This should have taught you that it is a crime to engage in partisan activities against the Soviet Union. Being properly educated, you are regarded as adults. That is why you have been punished as adults."

He then warned us that we had all come here to be punished, and that work was about to begin. He assured us that the administration knew how to run the camp, that they had means of finding out our most secret thoughts and plans.

5

The World of Prison Camps

APRIL 1949

The Dubrov area in which we were, formed only one of the many concentration camp centres in the Soviet Union. These were spread out across the entire country, as far north as the Kolyma Camps in North-Eastern Siberia, where gold was mined in the tundra. There was the Vorkuta region, also in the north, concentrating largely on anthracite mining; the Petchora region, in the north-east, with ordinary coal mines; the virgin forest area near Taiga above Lake Baikal, producing timber and asbestos; the Altai Mountains near Kazakhstan where quicksilver, copper and lead were mined. Farther south, was the Karaganda concentration camp area. There were further groupings, I believe, in Turkmenia and in the northern Caucasus.

All these other areas had a relatively healthy climate; whereas the Dubrov area was in the marshes, invaded by mosquitoes in summer and damp cold in winter. It had been chosen, as the ex-Tsarist officer had said, for the "political" prisoners, many of whom were often older men, incapable of the hard manual work required in the other, mining, areas. The work here was concerned largely with maintenance—bridges, roads, snow-clearing, or the unloading of railway wagons. The wagons arrived from the surrounding forests with timber for the other working camps in the Dubrov area, some of which

63

specialised in woodwork shops and furniture factories. While in quarantine, the work capacity of each of us was assessed by the *nariarchiks*, or inner camp administrators, and we were now allotted our place in working brigades.

These *nariarchiks* were the confidence men of the régime, selected from among the prisoners, usually Russians or men from the Soviet Union's other territories, who had been sentenced for some minor offence. They were exempted from outside work, and carried out administrative duties in the camp. They supplied the authorities with regular reports about the morale of the prisoners and other confidential matters. They were responsible for staffing the working brigades, to whom they forwarded orders received from the central officer. They were all loyal to the camp administration, and were always prepared to carry out any task, hoping for an amnesty, or at least for an improvement in their position, in reward for faithful service. This was a little naïve of them, because they should have known by now how the Soviet system worked, how little it cared about anyone who had lost its favour. But they obstinately clung to their hope of redemption.

One morning, a *nariarchik* came to our block with his adjutants, and allotted us to various working brigades, according to our fitness. The secret police made a final search of our barracks and then, after a month of quarantine, we came out into the working and, if one may so call it, the social world of the Soviet Concentration Camp 10.

We reported to our brigadier* who had received a list of names, and he gave us our tasks. Some of these

*The distinction between *nariarchik* and brigadier is, I hope, clear, as these terms will be frequently used. Both were prisoners in semi-official positions, the former administrative, the latter executive.

brigadiers were extremely unpleasant men; but ours, who was half Finnish, was helpful, even well disposed, to the Hungarians. He pointed out that our two nations, the Finns and Hungarians, were related, and he said he was glad I was working under him.

The day's work started with reveille at five in the morning when it was still dark. Breakfast lasted from half past five till seven, and was eaten first by the brigades going out to work. The invalid brigades employed on duties inside the camp went to the canteen after the muster roll, or *proverka*, had been taken, at seven.

This *proverka* was strictly observed, and everyone in the camp had to be present. Even the cripples (there were many in Camp 10) had to line up in the snow like everybody else, while the numbers were counted. Reports containing the exact figures were then telephoned to the central administration.

Breakfast and other meals were served in a wooden barrack hall with kitchen and pantries attached. We sat at long tables and benches, and the brigadier appointed men to bring us tin bowls of food. The system by which everyone went for food to the kitchen window had been tried, but it had not worked; some prisoners went twice while others obtained nothing. For breakfast, we were given a thin mush of half-hulled grain, and the daily bread ration of six hundred grammes. Some of us were so hungry that we ate the whole day's portion at breakfast.

After breakfast, the brigade leaders received their instructions for the day's work. We then went to the camp fences where an inner gate was opened, and we were admitted into the so-called "letting out" boxes. When the gates behind us closed, the gates of the outer fence were opened, and we went out. Outside the palisade, groups of armed guards with dogs were waiting for us, and after being counted again—we had to step forward in rows of five—we set off to work. We worked till half past twelve, and then had an hour's break. If we were near the camp, we went back for lunch; otherwise, our lunch was brought to us by the older, invalid prisoners. The afternoon shift lasted from two to six. In theory we did a twelve-hour working day; in practice, it was always several hours longer, either because special work had to be finished in time, or because we were delayed by the interminable countings and searchings.

Supper consisted of the same kind of mushy soup we had had at breakfast, and four or five *komsa*, a small salt fish two inches long sometimes called "Russian oyster", which was more nourishing. It was served between six and eight, usually to the old people before the working brigades returned.

One of our number, a medical man, calculated the calorific value of our rations. The invalids, he said, received 1200 calories a day, including the bread and the sugar ration; the workers, just under 1500. On paper it looked much better. The workers were supposed, officially, to receive 2800 calories a day; but by the time it reached them it was always below 1500. Corruption was so general that food was stolen at every stage in its delivery. The MVD, as well as camp administration, were guilty of this. The kitchen chef, the stock-keeper, the *nariarchiks*, all came in for their share too. There was no point in complaining, because prisoners were not trusted, nor were they expected to tell the truth. Some of the medical men among us said that the calories we received were half the minimum requirement under such conditions.

This under-nourishment was responsible for tuberculosis among the younger prisoners, as well as distrophea, a kind of slow starvation causing a gradual weakening of the body. They collapsed at work, and had to be taken to the hospital where they spent a few days on better food. In two or three weeks they would be back at work. There was a considerable traffic of this kind, people with distrophea continually going in and out of hospital. And we often saw the skeleton-like figures of the tubercular patients wandering about in the hospital enclosure, where they were allowed a little exercise. In summer, when their bodies were not hidden by clothes, their thighs looked as thin as ordinary people's shins. In the bath, I was once startled at seeing the protruding bones of my neighbour—only to realise that he was observing the exactly same phenomenon in *me*.

In the evenings, if we were not too tired, we tried to organise cultural groups to keep our minds occupied. The most popular occupation was learning foreign languages, especially English. This was, of course, strictly forbidden. English was the language of Russia's greatest enemies and, so the authorities argued, anyone caught learning it must hope for the victory of capitalism. Even Russian could not be studied because it might help prisoners attempting to escape. Any prisoner found trying to write Russian was punished with ten or fifteen days' *karker*.*

In spite of this threat, many prisoners risked the *karker* if they could pick up a few words of English. Many also studied French and German. I taught Hungarian to the Estonians and Lithuanians, who had a great talent for languages.

Some of the guards even wanted to learn foreign languages and, if it could be done secretly, we taught them. Miklos Csomos, my dentist friend, did not know much English, but he pretended to the guards that he was an expert, and was giving three of them lessons when

*A small underground cell, cold, damp and in semi-darkness, designed for special punishment.

we arrived. From time to time he invented completely spurious words to bedevil their efforts and would have to memorise them himself.

A Japanese metallurgical engineer called Okano also became a regular visitor to our barrack block because he wanted to learn English. He had been sentenced to twenty-five years' imprisonment for espionage. When the Russians arrived in Korea in 1945, they found that he knew too much about Korean politics to be left there, so they charged him with spying for the Americans. He was a shy man, but he became a part of our Baltic circle, and I believe he enjoyed it—if such a word can be used in a Russian concentration camp. We often used to sit together smoking a little squat pipe made from bread, which I had dried in an oven, handing it from one to the other and talking English. He told me about his metallurgical inventions, most of which were still in an experimental stage. He had most novel ideas about artificial fertiliser, and other chemical products.

Another friend was Harry Anderson, a Lett, who had lost a leg during the war, while fighting in the German Army.

After the war he visited a family in West Germany, in the American zone, to tell them of the death of their son who had died beside him in battle. They grew so fond of him that they adopted him in place of their son, and he married their daughter. All went well until the American secret service, who employed him on account of his knowledge of Russian, started sending him over to the Russian zone of Germany. His missing leg always helped him on these trips as everyone was sorry for him. But one day he was caught, and handed over to the Russians.

At the end of the day, *odboy*, that is Retreat, was sounded at nine, when everyone had to be by their

bedside. The staff came round and prisoners who were
not in their places were given *karker*.

One night we heard shots outside the camp followed
by snarling and growling. The experienced ears of my
fellow prisoners knew what this meant. Some wolves,
driven near the camps by hunger, had attacked the
watchdogs and torn them to pieces. We were delighted
to hear this because we hated the dogs. Trained to
hunt men, they were always loose at night along the
palisades, where they moved along wires to which their
chains were attached, giving them considerable freedom
of movement. If there was an escape they could alarm
the guards.

When I reached my new block after leaving quarantine,
the bunks were so crowded that we were unable to sleep
on our backs. We had to sleep on our sides, literally,
packed like so many sardines, all facing the same way
so as not to breathe into the neighbour's face. If in the
middle of the night you felt uncomfortable, you turned
round and woke him up; he, in turn, woke his neighbour
and so on until everyone was facing the other way. This
called for a good deal of tolerance, and a team of sleepers
had to be good friends.

A lot depended, too, on having neighbours who were
not disagreeable, from a purely olfactory point of view.
After having a number of dirty and very smelly sleeping
companions, I found Antonos Bruzhas, a Lithuanian, and
a most agreeable man with a good sense of humour. As
a boy he had been nearly executed at the time of the
Russian Revolution, because he used to turn the pages
for the organist in the local Catholic church.

It is often said that the only way to know someone
really well is to sleep with them—with all which that
implies. Of course the implications did not apply here,
although I shall have more to say about homosexuality

later. But by sleeping next to Bruzhas I got to know him very well.

Bruzhas had become a well-known figure in his country before the war, as the owner and editor of the biggest Lithuanian newspaper. Liberal and concerned chiefly with agriculture, it was the most popular newspaper among the small-holders and middle classes.

He used to laugh about this and say, "I wish I'd stuck to my organ playing. It doesn't get you into trouble like running a newspaper does. After we leave this place, I advise you, Raphael, to take a job in Hungary as a village organist. You'll be happy for the rest of your life."

As well as a sense of humour, Bruzhas was curiously fastidious and had a peculiar feeling for order and cleanliness. He told me that this had, on one occasion in 1918, saved his life. He had been taken for interrogation by the Communist Security Police who were then on the look-out for people with a "bourgeois background." The police station had two exits, one of which was filthy, the other relatively clean. The official finally got tired of questioning him and said, pointing to the dirty door, "All right, get out there!"

Bruzhas laughed and said facetiously, "No, it's filthy. I'd prefer to go through the other door. It looks cleaner."

The official said irritably, "Go where you like, you bloody bourgeois!"

Bruzhas afterwards discovered that the dirty door led to underground cells where prisoners were shot, while he had chosen the one into the street! "Things were like that in 1918," he said. "But they were very different when I was arrested this time, I can tell you."

Nevertheless because Bruzhas's family lived in Lithuania, he had the preferential treatment allowed to Russians, and he was allowed to receive parcels from home. In the last year, he had even been permitted to exchange letters twice a year with his family. The food parcels, which he generously shared with the rest of us, made a great difference to our lives. Even after years of Soviet occupation, the food parcels from Lithuania were still of good quality. The brigadiers generally expected a share of these Baltic parcels, and because I was Bruzhas's friend I, too, was treated better.

The start of our work fortunately coincided with the spring which lasts only a week or two, before the continental summer set in. These sudden changes of climate, from extreme cold to extreme heat, are most disagreeable when you are unaccustomed to them. But the sight of everything in bloom that first spring was inspiring, and we were glad to be out in the forests and fields. Such was the hunger of some of the prisoners that they cut the fresh grass, ground it with stones, put salt on it, and ate it. They claimed that it was full of vitamins. The other spring-time delicacy was the bud of the birch tree. When the guards were not looking, we descended on these like a cloud of locusts, denuding the trees of their buds as far as our hands could reach. We also picked and ate berries in the forest, and took some back to our older friends and sick prisoners in the camp.

There were other forms of nourishment which I found less attractive, cockchafers and various kinds of forest beetle. I even saw old people catching flies and eating them. For liquid refreshment, we drank the sap of the birch, the national tree of Russia. This was forbidden, but many of the prisoners had become very skilful in extracting the fluid. They made a small incision in the tree-trunk and tied a can below to catch it as it dripped out. It was thicker than water, and had a sweetish, not unpleasant taste. I am reminded here that among other equally curious forms of nourishment, prisoners often ate industrial vaseline. They spread it on the black bread, and persuaded themselves that it tasted like bacon dripping.

Miklos Csomos used to accompany us on these foraging expeditions and, as a medical man, he claimed to know all the vitamins. When I expressed my horror at the old men eating flies, he said, "They're much wiser than you. Flies are full of proteins. Don't think about it as you eat them. Chew them well, and they'll do you a power of good."

Sometimes while we ate these strange foods, Miklos would regale us with tales of imaginary Barmecide feasts. He had always been a great epicure in Budapest before the war, and he spoke of caviare and *boeuf Stroganoff* and *Saltinbocca alla Romana* and Château-Yquem and Chambolle-Musigny in such terms that our mouths watered. He would describe in great detail, the most superb banquets he intended to give himself when he got home from Russia. This over-optimistic approach to his future made us laugh at least. On one occasion we were able to satisfy even his gastronomic tastes. A covey of partridges, blinded by the sun, flew into our barbed wire one morning, leaving three dead against the palisade. These the camp baker prepared, cooked and shared with his friends. I have never enjoyed partridges so much before or since.

The guards who accompanied our working parties were uncouth men, whose motto roughly was, "Shoot first and ask afterwards." There had been a number of unnecessary shootings, especially in the cases of old feuds between a guard and a prisoner. This was why the infamous *zapret* or forbidden-zone system was introduced for working parties. A *zapret* zone was defined by notice boards, beyond which no prisoner might walk without permission. Equally, as long as the prisoner remained within the *zapret*, the guard was not allowed to fire at him—except, of course, in the case of a prisoner deliberately attacking a guard (many prisoners, apart from the bandits, were so desperate that they sometimes did this). Nor was the guard allowed to interfere with the speed or quality of a prisoner's work; these were the responsibilities of the brigadier. I mention these details in connection with a tragic incident which occurred not long after we started work.

One of my colleagues was a Ukrainian who was always taunting a guard we disliked. It was courageous, but it was also unwise, because the guard hated him, and was waiting to have his revenge. One afternoon the Ukrainian went into the *zapret* zone to relieve himself. He had presumably obtained permission, but as he was returning, we heard a burst of tommy-gun fire followed by a shriek—and there he was, on the ground, throwing himself from side to side, howling and bleeding. The guard had shot him down inside the *zapret* zone. We started to run to his help, but the guard shrieked that if we moved another step he would shoot us too. It was not long before the Ukrainian rolled over convulsively and was dead.

Another guard went off to fetch a truck and we were ordered back to work. Fortunately, most of the day's work was done, for no one felt like doing any more after this. A cart was brought from one of the collective farms, and the guards ordered us to lift the corpse on to it.

On the way back to camp, we were halted frequently, and the gaps between the marching columns were checked and widened. The spades, the only "weapons" we had, were collected and carried separately by three prisoners.

Such incidents in the past had led to bloody riots, and the guards were not taking chances. (Once when the prisoners were marching home after such an incident they had dragged the offending guard into their ranks, and finished him off with their hands.) We had to wait a quarter of an hour that evening before being admitted to the camp, where another reinforcement of armed guards had been called up, in case of trouble. Dogs were let loose inside, and we were confined to barracks. Later, we were allowed to go to the lavatories, but only in supervised groups, following a special route. No gathering of prisoners was allowed, and no one could leave his barrack block without permission. This was the first incident of its kind which I witnessed in Camp 10.

Later I had almost as unpleasant an encounter with a guard myself.

We had been ordered on to the railway, to unload a trainload of logs. While working in my wagon, I saw another brigade, composed chiefly of older men, trying to move a huge tree-trunk in a nearby wagon. They could not lift it and I went over to help; but my brigadier saw me and ordered me back to the wagon. As I turned to go, the brigadier in charge of the old man's brigade ran up behind and struck me on the head. As I had been only trying to help, I lost my temper and hit him back. When one of his colleagues approached me, I tripped him up so that he fell on the rails. There was a deathly hush. Everyone stopped work, waiting to see what would happen.

On these occasions, we were generally surrounded by a ring of guards pointing their tommy-guns at us; and one of the guards asked his officer for permission to shoot me. Fortunately Antonos Bruzhas, who could speak Russian, was standing near, and he immediately came to my rescue. He explained calmly to the officer what had happened, pointing out that I had been trying to help the old men, and had only acted in self-defence. He said he knew me, and that I was not the sort of man to start a brawl. He added—and this always impressed the prison authorities for some reason—that I had been on the staff of the allied forces during the war and had served with the British Army!

The officer asked if this was true. I said it was, and he told me to get on with my work. But the brigadier I had struck reported me to the camp authorities that evening. These offences were taken very seriously and I was sentenced to ten days in the *karker*. As it was summer this was not unbearable, but I decided after the first day to start a hunger strike. We found that this was a most effective device, because the Russians were, for some curious reason, nervous about hunger strikes. As they themselves are unable to resist food, or for that matter any of their animal or sexual urges, they thought that something very serious must be wrong with a prisoner who refused nourishment.

I was immediately taken before the camp doctor, a woman with the rank of captain. Helped by favourable reports from Miklos Csomos, who knew much more about medicine than she did, I was declared unfit for punishment and released.

I relate this incident with the guards, not only because I was involved in it, but because it also had its pleasant side, revealing the loyalty among prisoners. Had not Antonos and Miklos supported me at the risk of their lives I might well have lost my own.

6

The Bandits

I have already referred briefly to a feature of prison life which impressed me most strongly—the bandits. They were present in force in Camp 10, where they terrorised everyone, the guards included. They frightened the canteen staff into giving them extra food, and the medical staff into providing them with codeine, which they took as a stupefiant, together with alcohol and morphia. There was no point in complaining about them to the authorities, because they soon discovered who had denounced them, and the "traitor" might find himself strangled in his sleep, or with his throat cut.

The first incident which made me aware of them concerned the new chef in our canteen. This man courageously decided to stop the bandits' traffic with the *nariarchiks* and kitchen staff who gave them extra food, thereby reducing the other prisoners' rations. He paid dearly for this, because we saw him one day being chased by two bandits towards the hospital, with blood streaming from his head and neck. He only just reached the hospital door in time, and then collapsed. The orderlies dragged him in before the bandits could attack him again.

The bandits then tried to smash down the door; but the camp guards came running up, and the bandits then had the effrontery to go off to the *karker* where they cynically asked to be taken in, saying the punishment for their act would be two weeks' detention.

The bandits were great gamblers. Cards were forbidden, but they were ingenious in inventing other games of chance. They would play during the night, and to avoid trouble with the guards, would make little dummies from rags and old clothes, which they placed under the blankets so that their absence might not be noticed. Not only did they gamble with their own possessions, but with those of others. They would gamble, for instance, on who should rob an old man of a food parcel. The loser had to commit the theft. Sometimes a bandit who was not as heartless as his colleagues, would require the stimulus of a narcotic before he could commit a crime. If they could not get camp drugs, they would make their own *chihar*, which is a highly concentrated form of tea. They obtained tea from the frightened canteen staff.

If a "traitor" in the camp was to be punished, the execution of his punishment was decided by a game of chance. On one occasion, the lot fell on a bandit chief called Mussa, an oil engineer from the Caucasian mountains, who had a great reputation for toughness, and who could be relied upon to execute the sentence. His skull had once been cracked, so that there was an opening in his head, in which pulsating arteries were visible. The blow responsible for this had paralysed the left side of his body; but the right side was still very active.

The man to be punished was a Polish doctor who had refused to supply the bandits with drugs. Mussa put half a brick in a cloth bag and made his way into the doctor's barrack block. He then stalked up behind him unobserved, and hit him on the head with the bag. The skull was smashed, and the victim died on the spot. Mussa then went to the authorities and reported that he had killed a Polish doctor.

A court martial or trial was convened, purely, as far as I could see, for the sake of form. It was held in the canteen, and we were ordered to attend. It was the most cynical trial I have ever witnessed. The camp authorities smiled, the prosecutor smiled, the accused smiled, the audience smiled. And yet these smiles were concerned with the death of a human being! Mussa's penalty for murder was to start his twenty-five years' sentence over again.

The prestige of the bandit leaders was considerable. Frequently, if they told the brigadier of their working squad that they and their men would not work for the next few days, nothing was required of them. Sometimes the camp authorities showed a sense of humour. I remember on one occasion, a bandit chief telling his men not to work, and saying to the camp commandant, "After all, we've got twenty-five years ahead of us. There's time for everything, sir. Certainly for work!" The camp commandant thought this extremely funny; he roared with laughter and slapped the bandit on the back.

I must add a word about the self-mutilated prisoners, who were closely connected with the bandits. Indeed, most of the self-mutilated were bandits, for they were the only men who were tough enough to stand the pain. They had tremendous will power and knew enough of the régime to realise that there was no other way of escaping the slow and painful death by continuous overwork.

The self-mutilated in our camp were a horrible sight. They came mostly from the ice-fields of the north, from Vorkuta, Petchora, Kolyma, and other places with coal mines, where the work was the hardest in all Russia, and where railway lines connecting these places with the interior were being built with forced labour under appalling conditions. Most of the self-mutilation took place in the years immediately after the war, when the ration and clothing situation was worse even than now. In parts of Russia, in this northern tundra area, the inhabitants lived in greater poverty than the prisoners themselves, and starvation took a heavy toll among the ordinary civilian population. We heard this from Russian prisoners whose parents were among the victims.

Self-mutilation was carried out either with dynamite, or by making use of the new railways. A man would put his leg or arm on the rail and wait for the train. The best method in winter was to place the limb on the line and urinate on it. This froze it to the rail in a matter of seconds, as well as rendering it insensitive to the shock; but many men were so desperate that they could do it without even this home-made anæsthetic.

In our camp the prisoners without arms and legs were very poorly supplied with artificial limbs. A proper artificial limb was unknown in those days and they used sticks of wood which they had carved for themselves, attaching them with string to the stump.

In theory, criminals were separated from the political prisoners and put in their own camps. Why then did we political prisoners find the mutilated bandits so often in our midst? The answer is simple and frighteningly bureaucratic. By committing self-mutilation, a man sabotaged the labour system—and therefore became, automatically, a political offender.

One of the strange features of bandit psychology was their attitude towards the west. As these men were rebels against the Communist system (and the west was its enemy), they regarded Western ideas with something approaching veneration. This explains why we Europeans were not molested. Indeed, the bandits often helped us. As they knew the ways of the Communists and we, at the beginning at least, were ignorant of them, they offered to be our protectors, and warned us about the traps which would be laid by the camp adminstration. They also told us the names of the prisoners in front of whom it was dangerous to speak openly, the stool pigeons. They were quite ruthless with these men and considered it their duty towards the West to liquidate them. They were equally ruthless with any of their own circle who betrayed or deserted them, or disobeyed their orders.

But however well-disposed the bandits might be to Westerners, they always maintained a kind of closed shop attitude, guarding their innermost secrets most carefully, never allowing an outsider to enter into their thoughts or plans. It is unusual and surprising to find such an efficiently organised body of people among the Russians whom we Hungarians have always looked upon as hopelessly inefficient.

Although a man was once murdered in the bunk above my head, my own relationship with the bandits was amiable enough, because I was a European and therefore educated. In the early days however, they stole my shoes, my pipe and the tobacco pouch which the Japanese engineer, Okano, had made for me out of a few silk rags. But Bruzhas came to my rescue and would lecture the bandits on respecting my property. Perhaps because he had run a newspaper, he had a remarkable influence over these normally ruthless men and often succeeded in restraining them.

If a stool-pigeon suspected that the bandits might attack him, he would ask the camp authorities for a transfer. This was sometimes granted, but the result would generally be the same. News of his transfer would reach his new camp almost before he arrived, on the bandit bush-telegraph. Sooner or later they would have their revenge.

It was a long time before we discovered how the bush telegraph worked in this vast country, where there was no means of communication among towns, let alone among individuals. Some of the camp officers were former army officers, who considered that they were now serving in very inferior posts, and they were far from enthusiastic about the régime. Through these discontented camp officials, who naturally had means of finding out when a prisoner was being transferred to another camp, the bandits would obtain their information, which would be forwarded on in the same way through other discontented camp officials in the new camp.

The most remarkable example of the bush telegraph's effectiveness was the way in which twenty-eight isolated mines in the Arctic Vorkuta region went on strike simultaneously. But this is another story which I shall tell later.

7

Kaleidoscope of Nations

There were some three thousand prisoners in Camp 10, comprising an astonishingly heterogeneous selection of races; I counted twenty-eight nationalities. Fourteen were European; others came from the territories of the Soviet Union, but there were also Tibetans, Turks, Japanese, Lapps, Persians and Eskimos. At *proverkas* and mealtimes, a babble of different tongues arose from every corner of the hall and parade ground.

Of these groups, the people who impressed me most were the Balts. The inhabitants of the three little states on the eastern edge of the Baltic Sea, Lithuania, Estonia and Latvia, are to-day almost forgotten. It is quite wrong to look on them as under-developed people living on the fringes of European civilisation. Indeed, I now discovered that their knowledge of life and literature surpassed that of many other countries in Europe more favoured by nature and history.

They were the first to help newcomers when we still did not know our way about; they shared their food parcels with us, and claimed a kinship with the Hungarians, whose language and history they wished to learn. They told us how they, the Estonians, the Latvians, and the Lithuanians, who had not been the best of neighbours in the past, were now united against the common Russian enemy, that they had fought, and were still fighting, for their independence.

The West should know more about these brave people who have been resisting Russian Communism for the last two decades, a fight which has drastically depopulated them. Many of the survivors, including elderly people or children, are now being deported to distant parts of the Soviet Union to make way for new settlers from Russia itself. For as in the Ukraine, Bukovina and Galicia, the Communists know that the best way to deal with guerrilla warfare is to cut the partisans off from their sources of supply and information, the towns and villages which help them, by simply deporting the local population.

Many of the Balts in our camp had not been captured as partisans; they had been arrested in the towns and villages on trumped-up charges, generally for "collaborating with the fascists," which was ridiculous, for the Balts had fought the Germans as courageously as they now fought the Russians.

These hapless little nations have learnt a hard lesson during their history, which is one long succession of German and Russian occupations. A pathetic device they used against these two giant neighbours was to form local shooting units, or clubs, which could serve as a sports club in peace-time, and supply skilled marksmen in time of war. To belong to any of these clubs was now a criminal offence. But the Estonians and Latvians still have thousands of square miles of thick virgin forest, where the partisans have dug themselves underground shelters, and where a very few are still holding out. It was not difficult to obtain ammunition, because the retreating German army had left large supplies.

Later, in the spring of 1954, just before I left Russia, an Estonian doctor arrived in our camp, and told me that he had been operating with a unit of twenty partisans in the forests for the previous eight years. When I expressed surprise that this partisan warfare should still be going on, he said that fresh units were even then being formed in the forests. But their activities were becoming increasingly difficult because, with the arrival of alien and hostile Russian settlers, co-operation with the villages was harder.

I have said that these Baltic prisoners were regarded by the camp authorities as Russians, and were therefore allowed to receive letters from their families. But I wondered if this was really such a blessing. The letters always contained stories of family tragedies, of fresh deprivations and deportations. Some of the prisoners became demented when they received letters from their families who had been deported to the unknown virgin lands of Siberia. Others worried about news from their old parents. We considered ourselves lucky that we did not have to undergo this particular form of torture. If you have to be severed from your family for ever, it is better that the separation should be complete, that you should give up all hope of ever hearing from them again. We were told of a young Estonian engineer whose wife, thinking he was dead, married again. When she heard he was alive, she killed her two children and committed suicide. Then there were the two old Estonians who received news in a letter that their prisoner son was dead; they set fire to their house over their own heads, and then committed suicide. But they had received a false report. He was still alive.

These Balts were the most homogeneous of the groups in Camp 10, with the exception of course of the bandits, whose homogenity was created by common interests rather than common nationality. They did not look to the West for salvation. They remembered its behaviour during the Russian Revolution, and again in Hitler's time. Although the League of Nations had recognised their sovereignty, no action had been taken on their behalf by the major powers. When the Russians occupied their countries after the war, the West could do nothing. Although the Baltic States were on the agenda of the various international conferences which took place after 1945, Messrs. Truman, Eden, Bevin, Mollet, and the rest of the negotiators could not make Russia relent over Latvia and Estonia. "We are the stepchildren of Europe," one of them said to me. (I myself knew that Eden had done his utmost for them, and I tried to explain this.)

Whenever the Western enthusiasts in the camp started talking about the West, of how wonderful it must be to live there, of the coming Western liberation which would bring happiness to everyone, the Balts tried to disillusion them—not unpleasantly or bitterly, but simply by explaining that there was little to hope for, as the West would never start a war on their account.

One Lithuanian with whom I made friends had been Lenin's chauffeur just after the Revolution. He had gone about with Lenin everywhere, had eaten at the same table with him, and often slept in the same room. "We were happy in those days, with our new revolutionary freedom," he laughed. "I was young then. I was told, as were we all, that real life had just started. Freedom was round the corner. Lenin and his colleagues, I must say, behaved very decently. He was kind and thoughtful to his subordinates. He would turn in his grave if he knew what happened afterwards in the Soviet Union. He was so different from the ones that followed—he was cultured, well-read, a real gentleman."

I pointed out that this "real gentleman" had started the whole revolutionary horror. He now agreed that it had been a mistake from the start; that for the crimes which Stalin committed afterwards, Lenin, and his friends must bear a large part of the blame.

The next interesting racial group were the Poles. Everyone knows the tragic history of this brave people. But as a result of their sufferings, they proved better fitted than most races to stand up to the hardships of concentration camp life. Some of them had had the harshest experiences of all, in the Vorkuta mines where summer lasts only five or six weeks. In this extreme northern region of Russia there are no trees; the only vegetation is lichen, and even this is visible only for a short time in the summer. During the rest of the year snow, ice and frost cover the land.

The district of Vorkuta, the Poles told me, has a large network of concentration camps, and it produces the best anthracite in the Soviet Union. They were the first inmates of these camps, prisoners taken during and after the Russian invasion of Poland in 1939 and deported there, often by the most primitive means, on sledges. For over ten years they worked there, in the mines and on the new railways, in the worst possible conditions. It was a commonplace that, "under each sleeper of the railway to Vorkuta lies the body of a Polish soldier."

The supreme example of Polish bravery was revealed by the strike of Vorkuta miners organised in 1953. By then, they had reached such a state of desperation that they told their overseers they would no longer work in the mines and wished to go home immediately. When this demand was contemptuously refused, a young Polish colonel who had once been a fervent Communist, organised the strike in Camp 29. Within two days, all the mines in the Vorkuta area had stopped working. No one knew how the news spread, for the mines were far apart, in an almost uncharted region of Russia, and there was no means of communication between them. The coal supplies for the entire Leningrad industrial district which used mainly Vorkuta anthracite, were disrupted.

The Soviet authorities were so taken aback by this strike that they sent the Attorney-General and the Vice-Minister of the Interior to investigate. The prisoners of Camp 29 were assembled on the parade ground, and the Vice-Minister addressed them, asking them to state their requests. To the repeated demand that the strikers only wanted to go home, he replied with one simple, almost naïve, question, "But who will work here, if you don't?"

It was true; only forced labour could be used in such a climate. If that was the Poles' demand, he said, he refused to discuss the matter further, and he told them to go back to work. At this point, the prisoners to a man left the parade ground. The Vice-Minister of the Interior and the Attorney-General of the U.S.S.R. were left standing alone in the middle!

After this, not a mine in the district worked for ten days. The authorities erected loud-speakers all over the camp, and military music was played, interspersed with propaganda slogans and threats. Troops armed with machine-guns were brought up, and on the 1st August, the loud-speakers announced that if work were not resumed immediately, they would start shooting.

No one moved. And a few minutes later, the machine-guns opened fire on the barracks. A hail of bullets came in through the wooden walls, and within a matter of minutes there were two hundred and forty wounded and twenty-nine dead. Then came a pause in the firing, and further demands were heard over the loud-speakers. That was the end. In order to avoid further bloodshed, the Polish colonel ordered the prisoners to go back to work. The strike was over; he and the ring-leaders were arrested and executed.*

Another group in this kaleidoscope of nations with which I became friendly because, together with the Austrians, it was nearer to us Hungarians, was the German group.

The older generation of German prisoners still lived in a make-believe world of Kaiser Wilhelm II. Their happiest memories went back to before 1914, and they never stopped talking about the "good old days." They blamed the adventurous policy of Hitler for their miseries, claiming that he had upset the balance of Europe, bringing the Russian bear into Europe for the first time in history.

In curious opposition to them were the middle-aged Germans, most of whom had done well under Hitler in the boom created by his war industry. They, too, could not forget the good life they had known in the "thirties," and they reasoned in a curiously childish way. There was little point in arguing with them, particularly as their group contained a number of important Nazi officials including General Lombard, who had been one of Hitler's A.D.C.'s.

Lombard was an intelligent man, with a powerful personality; his influence on the younger Germans in the camp was so great that there was a permanent rift between them and the other nationalities. We tried to play down these differences, because we did not want the Russian authorities to watch the various groups of Westerners squabbling among themselves.

I worked side by side with General Lombard for two months, in the same brigade, loading tree-trunks; I even

*When I eventually reached England this was confirmed to me in 1958 by a Hungarian veterinary surgeon, Gaspar Szep, who was in Vorkuta at the time.

helped him at work, because his health was poor and he was weaker than the others. What appalled me most about this Nazi fanatic was that he still celebrated Hitler's birthday, annually. He would save up his bread ration for weeks; then, with a few Nazi friends, he would celebrate the great day with a bread orgy!

By one of the ironies of camp life, General Lombard's bunk neighbour had been Lenin's official interpreter, another fanatic, but this time a Marxist fanatic. Although diametrically opposed politically, these men were able to forgive one another their different ideologies; they even claimed to understand one another's points of view. But they could not forgive me for believing in Western liberal ideals.

Partly for this reason, I could not resist, one day, bringing Lombard together with a Jewish prisoner, an old man whose family had suffered greatly under the Nazi persecution. His eyes blazed when he learned who Lombard was, and all he could say to him was, "Look! Look! Just look what you Nazis did to us!" To which Lombard retorted automatically, "I'm sorry, but it was the law."

Lombard even tried to argue that the story of the liquidation of the Jews, the extermination camps and gas chambers was Allied propaganda. After a while, I gave up trying to discuss anything with such a bigot.

I only met one Englishman during the whole of my time in Russia, Alec Peters. He had been attached to the British military mission in Rumania and was about to sail for home in 1946, with his family from the port of Constanza, when he was arrested. The Russians had politely asked him to come ashore "just for two minutes," to deal with final customs formalities. These "two minutes" had so far lasted eight years. His family had sailed without him. He was quiet, dignified and courageous.

Then there were two American sergeants whose effervescent good humour helped to keep our spirits up. One of them said that what he regretted most in concentration camp life was "the lack of baseball." He even offered to teach us, "the best game in the world," when we returned to civilisation.

A more exotic, but equally representative, type of prisoner was the Spanish refugee from the Republican Army who, after fighting for the Communists in the Civil War, had fled to Russia, usually by boat or through France. He would ask for asylum in what he believed was the home of Socialism. But what did this home prove to be? After a few months, he and his fellow idealists had found themselves behind barbed wire.

I do not propose to speak of the French, the Austrians, the Dutch, and the other European races who were our fellow-prisoners, for they are familiar to most Western readers. But I must say a word about the multitude of races which make up Russia itself, many of whom are as dissimilar among themselves as we Westerners, Latins, Anglo-Saxons and Teutons are to one another. From the region of the Caucasus alone I counted fifteen different races. There were innumerable people from the Urals, and the Tartars in all their varieties, as well as the local inhabitants of the Dubrov area, the Chuvashes and the Mordvinians.

We had an Estonian ethnographer among us who explained that we were now living in the region in which our forefathers, and all the Finno-Ungrian peoples, spent a hundred and fifty years during their great migration from Asia, driven before the advancing Mongolian hordes. When they reached the European frontiers they divided into two streams, the Finns and

Estonians going north, while the other stream, the Hungarians, went south-west. As a Hungarian, I was fascinated to meet the Mordvinians, a people who did not pursue the migration as far as we and the Finns had. I often talked with these related races, trying to discover affinities in our languages.

Then there were the Armenians, the prisoners from Transcaucasia and Soviet Central Asia, the Azerbaianees, the Georgians, the men from Kazakhstan, Tadzhikistan, Uzbekistan, Turkmania and many other territories, all of whom formed different racial groups. It was difficult to get to know them, partly because of language difficulties, partly because we could not fully appreciate their peculiar Eastern mysticism; partly too because, in our presence, they lacked self-confidence. They seemed happy enough among themselves, and lived their own secluded lives without talking to anyone else. Nearly all were Mohammedans, calm and disciplined, meticulously practising their rites and saying their prayers regularly at daybreak and sundown, under the direction of their muezzins. The Soviet authorities tried to discourage this, but without success. Indeed, I learn that the persistent devotion of these peoples is to be found in all the camps of Russia. At first they did not know who we were and were suspicious, but the initial timidity gradually disappeared, and we later had many opportunities of experiencing the generosity of these half-Asiatic Russians towards us Westerners. The same could be said of the Buddhists, with whom we quickly made friends.

There were a number of Tibetans, and a multitude of Far-Eastern peoples, whose names are still unknown to me. One of their lamas, a civilised man, skilled in the ancient medical practices of his land, tended the sick of every nation. He spoke French and introduced us to two Mongolians from Ulan-Ede near the Baikal Lake, who had been condemned to fifteen years' imprisonment for "incitement and propaganda." He remarked ironically that he could not imagine them inciting anyone; they were so uneducated that they could barely pronounce their own names. They had of course not been tried, but arbitrarily arrested and brought here.

The lama was most touched when I pronounced the familiar incantation of his language, *Omane padne hum*. He made deep obeisances, embraced me, and even presented me with one of his few possessions, an old wooden Mongolian pipe. I treasured this for months, until it went the way of all personal possessions, stolen by the bandits.

Many groups of younger Russians had been brought up without religion, Eastern Ukrainians, White Russians and some of the Tartars. They lacked the moral fibre of the others; but they too soon learned to adapt themselves to the general atmosphere of the camp, to feel pity at the sight of suffering. Unaware of what they were doing they had adopted the Christian principles—"Thou shalt not steal!"—"Thou shalt not kill!"—"Thou shalt love thy neighbour!"

As well as these religious and ethnological groupings of the Soviet peoples, there were also political distinctions. First, came the old generation of Russians, including a number of officers who had served in the Tsar's army. They were nearly all over seventy, and had been brought up in the Christian religion, which had left its mark. It was with these older Russians who spoke French and German that we had most in common.

After them came the generation of early Communists, now mostly in their late fifties, the first supporters of the 1917 revolution, who had believed fervently in Lenin and in the future of Communism. They were now disillusioned, for they had learned during those terrible days in the thirties that it was enough to declare oneself a follower of Lenin to be condemned without trial.

Within this last group were sub-divisions: the old revolutionaries who still considered themselves good Socialists, declaring that the Stalinists were heretics and criminals, who had besmirched the sacred name of Communism; and then a large group of older Communists who had simply become disillusioned with the whole movement, and who now no longer believed in anything. Having not been brought up as Christians, knowing no other religion or philosophy save Communism, they wandered about in a mental void, and spoke bitterly against everyone and everything.

There was also a group of ex-Stalinists, former secret police or army officers, government officials, even ministers, who had become victims of personal intrigues, or sectarian quarrels; they too had been imprisoned without having ever seen the inside of a law court. A private report had been enough to imprison them; the big black car had come in the middle of the night, and their families had seen them no more.

Another Russian group consisted of ordinary workers and peasants who had been sentenced for stealing government property, having not earned enough to support their families. They told us the new Russian proverb, "He who doesn't earn enough to live, steals the rest." There was not, they had to admit, much to steal, a few pounds of flour, a sack or two of potatoes, some cabbage. They told us of mounds of corn, which, for lack of storage facilities, were left about in the open where, after months, moss grew on them, and thousands of roubles worth of food rotted. Yet, if they stole one pound from this they would be sentenced to fifteen years' imprisonment.

Finally, there was the large mass of rank and file

Russian soldiers who had fought in the Second World War. In some ways, they were the saddest group of all. They had seen the West, where they had begun to appreciate the higher standard of living, the better working conditions, higher pay and other amenities which they had been taught did not exist outside Russia. When they returned to their villages after the war, relating told what they had seen, they were sentenced for "spreading enemy propaganda." One Russian soldier had told his friends that the American Studebaker military trucks were more reliable than the Soviet Zis trucks. For this he was given fifteen years' hard labour.

Tragic too was the case of the Russian soldiers who had been sentenced simply because they had been taken prisoner by the Germans. They had been told to fight to the last, in the event of capture to commit suicide. I talked to one of these, who said: "I was separated from my family for four years. During that time we fighting soldiers did not receive letters or parcels from home—not to speak of leave. I was wounded three times. Instead of sending me home to recover, they sent me to the front to fight on—and bleed on—for the victory, the glorious victory of the Soviet Union. I was captured because I could hardly walk. Now at the end of the war, this is my reward."

Another Russian soldier who had lost both his arms in the war was taken prisoner, and afterwards charged in Russia with treason for not having shot himself. "But how could I?" he cried indignantly. "I had no hands to shoot with!"

There was also a group of Russian soldiers who had contracted venereal disease in the West during the war. They had been sentenced for sabotage!

One soldier told me he could never forget what he had seen in Europe. "I now know it is to Europe that we belong," he said. "And if we fought again, it would be to establish contact with Europe, to join her community. I now know that everything we are taught here, the system under which we grew up, the perfection and superiority which we hear so much about, the things we fought for with such enthusiasm—it's a pack of lies."

Russian soldiers like this man soon found there was something to be said for the European prisoners, and became our friends. Together with the bandits, who also knew the Soviet world so well, they often helped us in our troubles with the camp authorities, particularly when we had to appear before them for interrogation. MGB officers would appear unexpectedly in the middle of the night, and question us individually, demanding information about the general mood of the camp, or about a particular prisoner. Sometimes they would ask for a deposition against a friend who was still in the West, on the basis of which he could be arrested or kidnapped. From our Russian friends we learnt the necessary duplicity, the way to reply, to tell our lies plausibly, and thus avoid disaster for those distant friends, as well as for ourselves.

8

Women's Camps

In the first years after the war, there were several camps in the Dubrov area where men and women were imprisoned together. Later, they were divided into separate camps; but the two sexes still often found themselves working together, principally where technical rather than manual labour was required, in the power stations, machine-workshops, hospitals and bakeries.

In ordinary life, it is the man who makes the advances, and the woman who appears shy and uninterested. In our camp it was the other way round. Although biological factors may have played some part in this, there was another, a more practical, reason for this uterine frenzy. By having a child, a woman could be sure of two years of comparative ease. She was looked upon as its "guardian," and did not have to work, because it stayed with her in a maternity camp. As the state considered itself a kind of father or guardian to these children, and attached great importance to their upbringing as future Communist citizens, considerable material aid was given to the mother during the first two years. Then suddenly, on its second birthday, the child was snatched away and placed in a kindergarten, weaned as it were, after the manner of a lamb or a calf. The mother then returned to ordinary camp life, where she quickly searched for further fornications, in the hope of another pregnancy.

Sexual intercourse therefore took place whenever possible; behind the factory benches, in the lavatories, in the fields, above all in hospital. This was a further reason why prisoners were always trying to go to hospital. The younger ones, in whom the sexual urge was strongest would do almost anything to get there, from feigning illness and poisoning themselves, to swallowing needles, buttons, spoons, and in some cases deliberately mutilating themselves. Once inside the hospital, discipline was not strict, because the prison doctors had their mistresses, and the camp administration did not wish to lose the few good medical men they had, and upon whom the health of the whole camp, the guards included, depended.

One young German prisoner used to climb into the hospital to make love to a nurse in a private room, on a bed. How he managed this princely luxury, I do not know. He was tall, blond, blue-eyed and good-looking, and one day some nurses who had heard all about his prowess contrived to watch him surreptitiously through a window. It was evidently such a masterly performance that they lost all self-control, broke into the room, caught hold of him and refused to let him go.

By now a number of other nurses had arrived on the scene, and the problem was how could one man possibly satisfy the craving of so many sex-starved women? One of the older nurses hit upon a brilliant idea; she had heard that a piece of twine tied round the base of the male organ would keep it erect. This was done, and all the ladies were satisfied. It was only fair to add that the young man had to be carried back to his barracks on a stretcher afterwards. He never visited the hospital block again.

The palisades which divided men and women in the hospital quarters were not closely supervised, and anyone caught climbing over them generally received only a minor punishment; but such was the sexual desire of some of these prisoners, that they would even dig trenches under the fences. It was not unusual for twenty men to have intercourse with one woman in the same night.

When the vigilance of the guards made it impossible for the men to reach the women, they contrived artificial insemination. The women would throw phials or small bottles, which they had stolen from the ambulance or the doctors' consulting room, over the palisade to some co-operative male. If a woman was found to be pregnant she would receive only a small punishment, for the Russians needed these new citizens.

Prisoners who visited, or worked in the women's camps, told me they had seen the bodies of small babies, only a few months old in an embryo state, in the lavatories. Until a pregnancy is five or six months old it is not visible, and the women had to continue working although they were pregnant. Suddenly cramps and labour pains would come on, and the only relatively private place to which they could escape was the lavatory. Here they would have their miscarriages.

Abortion was less frequent, and then chiefly for women who had husbands and children at home, and who were serving a sentence of not more than five or six years. They hoped that, sooner or later, they would return to ordinary life, and they were ashamed of having become pregnant through some chance encounter. But there were also unmarried girls who, during their early pregnancies, decided they did not want their baby; they too were ashamed, and often performed their own abortions, using the most primitive instruments.

It is strange how youth, even overworked and undernourished youth, knows no sexual barriers, and will go to any length to satisfy the biological urge. When conditions improved after 1953 with better rations, and the Red Cross food parcels began arriving from abroad, this sexual craving became a mania, causing on one occasion a mutiny in the women's camp. They put down their spoons in the dining-room and started a hunger strike. It lasted days—a hunger strike for men. They shouted in chorus, "Bring us men! Men! Men!!!" Finally, the commandant himself had to go in to calm them. He was a humourless man and he only irritated them with his bureaucratic jargon. "This is an ungrantable wish," he said. "According to the latest administrative orders of the Soviet Union the sexes are to be segregated. It is not within my jurisdiction to alter orders."

While he was saying this, one of the women, who was a prostitute, ran forward, tore off her clothes, and offered him her naked body. "If you can't provide us with proper men," she cried, "we'll have to make do with you, Commandant. Take me!"

Women prisoners often behaved more grossly than the men because many were *blatnoi* girls—that is, a particularly low type of Russian woman, virtually a whore. At that time, the term "teddy-girl" had not been coined, but it would probably describe them to-day. They were shameless, often as ruthless in satisfying their wants as the bandits. Many of them were real prostitutes, whom the Soviet authorities proudly announced had been banished from the Russian streets.

An embarrassing type of female prisoner was the prison barber, (women tended to take over the less strenuous services). We were shaved every week, not only our beards but, as a precaution against lice, our bodies. As can be imagined, this gave the *blatnoi* girl barber countless opportunities for obscenities. I remember one young priest who became very embarrassed while his body was being shaved. "Don't worry, Father," she cried, "I'll do you well, but in return, I want to have you. You have *such a good one!*"

Sexual life for the miners in the far north, in the Vorkuta mines for instance, was different. These prisoners had better treatment because their work was essential and they were so remote, many thousands of miles from civilisation, where there was no opportunity for escape. They had better food, and were even allowed to consort with the free Russians living in the neighbourhood, and visit their families. It was inevitable that sexual relations in such relative freedom should take place, and many illegitimate children were born. Later, after 1953, when the Soviet Union began to grant amnesties to foreigners, allowing them to return home, I heard of many Hungarian miners who were accompanied back by their "partners in life", (using that phrase in its natural meaning), and their Russo-Hungarian children.

On one occasion during this repatriation period, a group of new prisoners arrived in our quarantine buildings. They were mostly Russians, but there was also a Hungarian woman among them. I waited for an opportunity in the evening to talk to her through the palisade.

She was beautiful, with an oval face and brown hair. She made a sign to me as she came to the palisade and asked despairingly: "Are you Hungarian?" When she heard my voice, she clutched the bars and began weeping. She said she had not heard a word of Hungarian for six years. Her name was Countess Maria Szechenyi; she came from Eotvos Puszta, and was the daugher of Count Paul Szechenyi, a member of one of the oldest families of Hungary. We found we had many friends in common.

After this, thanks to the help of an Estonian doctor we were able to exchange letters, and even meet, quite frequently. I came to know her well.

Then one day, the order came for her to move to another camp. I did not sleep the whole of that night, and I waited about outside the departure building in the early hours of the morning. When she came, she said she had been given dried food for five days, which generally meant a long journey east; she said she knew she was bound for Siberia. I tried to console her, telling her that they would probably take her to Lvov, the repatriation camp, and that she would go back to Hungary. I told her that whatever happened, I would not forget her; I would trace her and not let her die. She made the sign of the Cross and left, crying desperately in those last minutes.

Later I heard that her fears were justified; she was deported to Siberia. When I complained about this to the camp authorities, I was told: "Her aristocratic origins made her a particularly difficult case." Could there be a more bureaucratic way of describing banishment to one of the most notorious places in the world?

The most brutal affair I heard of during the whole of my time in the camps also took place in hospital. It was early after the war, in 1945 or 1946, when conditions were deplorable and prisoners were dying of hunger. At this time the authorities employed free Russian personnel from outside, among whom was a woman doctor. She was fat and well proportioned, and one evening she was attacked by a group of famished prisoners, probably bandits, as she was returning home after work.

As the woman passed one of the barrack blocks, they grabbed her and pulled her inside. These barracks were built on piles, and between the floors and the ground, was an empty space. The woman was dragged into this, where she was raped. But this was not their main interest. Such was their hunger that they killed her, chopped her up, and cooked her over a fire made of the loose planks. They ate her and burnt the bones.

Western prisoners who had heard about this did not want to talk about it, but we were introduced to one Westerner who had unwittingly taken part in this horrible feast. He had been told it was dog meat, and the other prisoners advised us not to tell him the truth. Later, he did discover it and was ill for weeks.

I have mentioned that not all the sexual relations in the camp were heterosexual. It was the westerners, the Germans, Danes, Dutch, the so-called civilised nations, who practised homosexuality. To the Russians, Balts, Czechs and Slavs generally, this habit is alien; and I came across only one Hungarian male couple. Homosexuality was easier to practise, of course, than normal love, and the men who did so were quite shameless about it, sleeping together in their bunks, in front of us all. I remember a German couple in our barracks who had been together for three years. When they were separated, and sent to different camps, they were in tears. We almost felt sorry for them.

In short, concentration camp life had many strange effects on the sexual behaviour of prisoners, of which I shall have more to say later.

9

Self-Made Doctors

I hope I have not given the impression that a camp hospital was only attractive for the sexual amenities it offered: we all wanted to be there for a variety of other good reasons.

In case of illness, a serious, if ineffective, attempt at diagnosis and cure was made, and the hospital was divided into several sections, like any Western hospital, for abdominal diseases, contagious diseases, a surgery, a dispensary, and so on. But the equipment was so primitive and the doctors and *feldshers,** so ignorant, that they were seldom effective. There could be no better proof of this than the delight of the camp authorities when a European doctor or dentist, like Miklos Csomos, arrived as a prisoner. He would be immediately seconded for hospital duties, where he would have no more faithful and devoted patients than the members of the camp administration, the MVD officers, their wives and children.

Indeed, any camp possessing a European doctor or dentist considered itself fortunate, because his knowledge was far superior to that of his Russian colleagues. There was always a procession of free Soviet citizens (Mordvinian peasants from outside the camp), in the corridors and waiting-rooms of these western doctors, who were also taken outside the camp under armed escort to

*Feldsher—a kind of high category male nurse used, particularly in the Russian Army and in rural areas, as a physician.

perform operations on the free Russians in their homes. The European doctor prisoners lived under rather better conditions than we did, but they had more work than they could perform, at all hours of the day and night. They often saw their patients die for lack of proper medical equipment and drugs.

In Tsarist times the best Russian doctors could, it was said, be compared not unfavourably with European doctors. But after the Revolution, when thousands of trained medical men were liquidated with the rest of the bourgeoisie, or fled abroad, or were imprisoned, the medical system broke down. Russian doctors who had spent ten or fifteen years in a concentration camp (as some of ours had), had been cut off from the progress of medicine. They were fully aware of this, and they did their best to catch up, watching our European doctors at work. In some cases they succeeded, because their original training had been good.

One of the younger Russian doctors told me of the extraordinary examination system by which medical students qualify in Russia to-day. At the end of the fourth year, they are divided into groups, and each group appears before a jury. This jury treats the students rather as a business-man treats a sample; he picks one here, one there, examines it, and makes his decision to buy or not to buy. In the same way the jury picks out one or two students from the group, asks them a few questions, and they judge the level of medical knowledge of the whole group on the basis of their answers. If eighty students appear before a jury, approximately seven or eight are examined. If they pass, all eighty pass; if they fail, all eighty fail. Many of these young Soviet doctors were ashamed of their ignorance, and they worked hard to learn. The European doctors considered it a duty, and often a pleasure, to teach them. In the evenings Miklos Csomos would hold classes for them and the *feldshers*.

The *feldsher* system, which is unknown in the West, dates from the Middle Ages, when the *feldsher*, a cross between a barber and a "sawbones," cut, bled, operated and, with any luck, cured. The modern Soviet *feldsher* had to undergo a two-year course in nursing and medicine. Later, I believe, the course was extended to three years, but it was still superficial enough. They were taught to give first aid, injections, to bandage wounds, nurse, prescribe simple medicines, and diagnose the more common diseases.

Most of the hospital staff in Camp No. 10 were conscientious, well-meaning and humane. Even the most stony-hearted Russians were sooner or later moved by the suffering they saw on every side. But there were some unscrupulous *feldshers*, who levied taxes on the older and more helpless prisoners. To be nursed properly, these poor old people had to pay a bribe, in the form of their clothes, food, tobacco, or other private property. When the sick were moved from their barracks to the hospital, they took along their personal belongings in a sack, which was kept in the hospital storerooms. These sacks were easy prey for the hyenas (as we called the bad *feldshers*), who divided the treasure among themselves, so that they should all be involved, and no one could betray the others.

The belongings of those who died in hospital were immediately appropriated by the hospital staff, just as the effects of those who died in the barracks were automatically inherited by the Soviet state—that is by the camp administration and the MVD officers. We often noticed a pair of gloves, a scarf, or some other piece of clothing which had belonged to a dead friend being worn by the guards.

The camp pharmacy occupied one room in the hospital, and was run by a trained Russian pharmacist who was not a prisoner. In our hospital, there were two young Russian Communist girls, free Russians, employed as his assistants. Our doctor told us that they had to watch them very carefully to prevent mistakes because, though some of the pharmacists were reasonably well trained, these two were very ignorant.

Fortunately, the pharmacist could not cause much harm because the drugs were of very poor quality and ineffective. But in the case of heart trouble, the size of the dose was important. Digitalis, for instance, is an excellent heart medicine, but its application requires precise knowledge. In our camp, the pharmacists distilled it from dried foxglove leaves, and the strength of the drug depended on how much they put in the water. Sometimes it was too strong; sometimes, it was not strong enough; sometimes, it did not act at all.

Western training was held in such esteem that it was enough if a prisoner had spent a year in a Western medical school, even as an unqualified student, for him to be immediately appointed to an important post in the hospital. Once there, he stayed indefinitely. As time went on, the status of these European medical men increased, to the point that they were able to order their own drugs and medical books, and work on their own. So anxious were the authorities to employ Europeans with even the most rudimentary knowledge of medicine that some preposterous situations arose.

A Hungarian friend of mine, Martin Schneider, a forestry engineer and a witty fellow, one day told his brigadier that he could not work because he was ill. The brigadier took him to the *feldsher*, who asked what was wrong.

"I have piles," said Schneider.

It was the only complaint he could think of which the *feldsher* might not care to examine. Unfortunately the *feldsher* was conscientious, and he made him take down his trousers and bend over. He examined him and then declared that Schneider was shirking; he had no piles.

"What! No piles!" said Schneider. "You're telling me. *I, who am a doctor?*"

The *feldsher* was taken aback. "You, a doctor!"

" Of course," replied Schneider unwisely.

" Wonderful! Marvellous! You don't know how good that is. We're terribly short of doctors. We've been hoping all along that some more European doctors would turn up and give us a hand."

With that the *feldsher* hurried off to the camp administration, with the result that, a few minutes later, Schneider found himself before the commandant who, after a few questions, ordered him to take over the convalescent wards, and hold a nightly clinic.

Schneider was frightened out of his life; he said he didn't know whether to laugh or cry. Being a doctor was a responsible job, and he was afraid that he might kill someone. He had had some first aid training in the army during the war, it was true, but that was years ago. They took him to the camp hospital and told him to get to work right away, that very night.

Among the older patients were a number of Hungarian officers who were delighted at last to have a real Hungarian doctor to look after them. They hoped that this would improve their lot, because doctors could do a great deal for their patients, not only for their health but also—which was almost as important—for their diet. Schneider decided to tell them the truth; he said he was a forestry engineer, not a doctor. He asked their advice. They were highly amused.

"Keep on playing the doctor," they said. "However

ignorant you are, you'll certainly do it better than these wretched *feldshers*!" If he were clever, they said, he could not only help himself by getting a soft job in the hospital, but also his fellow countrymen, who were trying to recuperate there. Being familiar with conditions in the hospital, they said that a Hungarian with resourcefulness, daring and bluff could get away with almost anything.

After some misgivings, Schneider agreed. He possessed all the wit and daring in the world, and he played his role as well as he could. He looked after his patients, obtained vitamin pills for them, and persuaded the camp administration to improve their food. Fortunately, he had a German male nurse working under him who had already spent two years in the camp, and who could recognise most of the ordinary symptoms. He could speak and write Russian, and he acted as Schneider's interpreter. Without this interpreter, Schnieder would have been lost.

Before the war Schneider, as a Hungarian of German extraction, had often visited Germany, and he had served with the German Army during the war. This helped him now, because the interpreter trusted him, almost as one German would another. Schneider told him what had happened, and they organised the work accordingly. For some months they worked without a hitch, while Schneider learnt how to use the stethoscope, how to examine chests and rectums, in short how to behave as a qualified doctor.

One day he received a message that the chief medical officer of the Dubrov camps wanted to see him and put him through a higher examination. Schneider was terrified, but he still had a few days left to study. He had made friends with a Lithuanian doctor who worked in another section of the hospital, to whom he again confessed his ignorance. This doctor had helped him solve problems of anatomy and pharmaceutics before; and Schneider now studied with him so well that he came out of the examination with flying colours—and was told to go on with his work.

All went well again until a new batch of prisoners arrived from Europe, among whom was the chief assistant at the Department of Internal Diseases in the Berlin University Clinic. When the camp administration learnt who this German was, they immediately appointed him to the hospital, and ordered him to report to the chief medico, Dr. Schneider, under whom he was to work. The Berlin specialist said he would be delighted to work with a Hungarian doctor. He hurried off to the hospital to find Schneider.

Schneider turned red, then white, when he learnt who the new prisoner was. Once again, he decided to tell the truth; he called the German into his office and put the problem squarely to him. The Berlin doctor took the whole thing with great good humour and told Schneider to stay where he was; they could work quite well together, he said. He would examine the patients, and tell Schneider what to do. In this way, they would be able to do even more than Schneider had before for the patients. (I should mention here that Schneider was not an unscrupulous man; he would not have looked for this soft job to take it from another doctor. There were simply no other doctors then in the camp.)

Schneider and his new "assistant" worked together admirably for a while, but Schneider's conscience started to trouble him, and he was constantly wondering how to extricate himself from the situation. He was also afraid of being found out. Finally, before he could do anything more, he fell extremely ill, with pneumonia and pleurisy. There was no penicillin in the camp, and very few sulphonamides. It was fortunate that he was a "doctor," because being in the hospital his trouble was soon diagnosed, and his colleagues were able to obtain extra food and medicine for him.

For a long time he hovered between life and death, but he finally recovered. He then made the excuse that he was too weak to fulfil his duties as a physician, and he left the hospital, to be finally transferred with a group of prisoners to the Vorkuta coal-mining region, where he worked as a machinist.

This was not the only case of its kind. In the Dubrov camp area, where I spent the greatest part of my captivity, there were many Germans and Hungarians who had never been physicians but who held medical positions; they too were clever and conscientious.

Among these was my friend Istvan Szabo, who had been a medical student at Debrecen for a year until the war, when he became an active officer in the Hungarian armoured corps. He was captured in 1945, at the siege of Budapest, and taken to Russia, where a military tribunal sentenced him to twenty-five years' imprisonment as a war criminal. In 1948 he was brought to the Dubrov area.

He took his medical studies very seriously and found several well-trained European physicians, who were only too glad to help him. They taught him and found him more useful and reliable than the Russian *feldshers*, or even the Russian physicians. In the eleven years he spent in Russian concentration camps, he studied systematically, first from the extensive notes dictated to him by these European doctors and, in the last four or five years, from the medical books he was allowed to read. He worked in various hospitals, including the central hospital of the Dubrov area, and in the northern camp areas, as general practitioner, surgeon, and later as dermatologist. He even performed appendicectomies and rib resections. When the Hungarian prisoners were sent back to Hungary, he accompanied them as their doctor. Yet he had never passed an exam in his life!

Another Hungarian whose name I will not mention because he is still alive in Hungary, had been an airman, and he had no medical knowledge at all. When, by chance, he became a hospital nurse in Camp No. 9, he did so well that he soon became a head nurse, then section head, and finally he was appointed medical examiner in charge of all autopsies. (After 1949-50 the prisoners who died were taken to Camp No. 9 for autopsy. Before that, they had been buried on the spot, because the authorities were indifferent about the cause of their death.)

Sometimes, he said, mysterious corpses were brought in from outside the camp by MVD, or by army personnel who did not belong to the camp administration. They would swear my friend to secrecy, make him perform the autopsy, and then write down his findings in their presence. He always knew when a body had been brought in from outside, partly because he would have recognised it if it had been a fellow prisoner, partly because most of them were shot in the nape of the neck, the standard Russian form of execution. He did his work efficiently, became an expert in anatomy, and it was only in the last years, on account of some love affair, that he was dismissed and sent back among the ordinary prisoners.

Another good Hungarian friend, Dr. Gyorgy Halasz, who was really an agronomist and had studied a little veterinary surgery, pretended to be a physician, and found himself one day doing his first autopsy. He was an intelligent young man, as skilful as Schneider in fooling the Russians. His first autopsy was on a man who had been beaten to death by the bandits. Because it was a camp murder, all the free medical officers of the camp area were present (although they made a prisoner do the dirty work).

Dissection for autopsy is always begun under the chin. But Halasz, being ignorant, took the plunge and stuck his dissecting knife into the corpse's belly and cut open the bowels, so that their contents spattered all over those standing around watching the autopsy. He then cut the body in pieces as one might a dead dog or a cat—and all the time he dictated his findings in German to his Estonian assistant. He used veterinary terms, not ordinary human ones, but behaved with such assurance that it did not occur to the Russian doctors that he was an impostor. One of the Russian physicians even remarked quietly to another that it was very interesting to compare the difference between the Russian and the European methods of dissection!

The best organised and most successful branch of medicine in the concentration camps was surgery. When there is a shortage of medicines and drugs, there is a natural tendency to put faith in the scalpel. Our doctor friends and patients told us about these operations, which were often performed without anæsthetic. I had a friend, a Hungarian barber from Veszprem, who suffered from stomach ulcers. One of these was perforated, and an operation was necessary. He was taken to the central hospital, and a Russian surgeon operated on him. This doctor was the chief of the surgical department, not a prisoner, but a free man. My friend told me that the operation lasted three hours without anæsthetics, and he was in terrible agony. But the Russian doctor said, "Be patient, be brave, my friend, you are a Hungarian. Hungarians can stand anything, because you are the toughest fellows on earth."

My friend told me how conscientious this doctor was. He had two operations to perform that day, but he did not go home between them; he lay down for a while on a bench in the corridor, to prepare for the next. On other days, he would visit his patients almost hourly. Everyone spoke of him with gratitude and admiration. He belonged to the MVD organisation, it was true, but he considered himself a physician and surgeon first.

There was another famous Moscow professor in the camp who, as a result of some intrigue, had been sentenced to ten years' imprisonment. He even performed brain operations. We also had a throat specialist, an outstanding European doctor, who performed a number of ear and mouth operations. There were some experts on nervous diseases, and a mental section for lunatics. This section was always overcrowded, for many of our unfortunate companions had gone out of their minds.

While on the subject of surgery, I must pay tribute to a Viennese physician of Ukrainian origin, Dr. Zderovich, who in his youth had been assistant to the world-famous Professor Chvostek, the founder of modern diagnostics at Vienna University. He was reputed to have performed miracles, not only on the prisoners, but also on the free workers outside the camp. One night, he was taken to a woman with a perforated appendix, and he operated on her successfully by candlelight, using only a knife, in most unsanitary conditions. Zderovich was a wonderful man, whose name will always be remembered with gratitude by thousands of prisoners. Thank God he is still alive to-day, back at his good work in Vienna!

As far as dentistry was concerned, there was, needless to say, only one treatment: extraction. Later corruption, acting this time in favour of the prisoners, enabled the dentists to lay hands on one or two drugs and some drilling equipment. Those who had to be treated first with it were the MVD personnel, the civilian and military administration, and the free Russians living outside the camp. Whenever a European dentist like Miklos Csomos appeared, the camp authorities spared no efforts to obtain instruments for him.

As soon as Miklos arrived, he immediately set to work on the prisoners' mouths, and found that many of the older men had lost most of their teeth. It was impossible in those first years to obtain false teeth, but during my last year in the camps anyone with money could buy them, at least in the central and industrial camps. The camp administration turned this into a most profitable little private enterprise, demanding far more money for the false teeth than the cost of the raw materials, while the prisoners had to make them up for nothing.

During the early days in Camp 10 my own teeth came in handy, in a very strange way. We had been through another of the diarrhoea epidemics which periodically struck our camp, and we were all feeling very weak. We needed cod liver oil and vitamins, and we had heard that one of the pharmacists, a free Russian girl called Komsomolka, had some to sell. As there was corruption in every walk of Soviet life, you could generally obtain anything if you paid.

Fortunately Miklos discovered that the Russian girl wanted a gold tooth, for which she said she would exchange her cod liver oil. But where could the gold be found? We discussed this at length, and then I remembered that I had a gold crown on one of my back teeth. I suggested that Miklos might take it off. He tried but it proved impossible to prise it away with his primitive instruments. I told him to extract the tooth. "God knows," I said, "how long we shall go on living on *kasha*. For that I don't need any teeth!"

Neither cocaine nor local anæsthetic existed of course, so I gripped the arm of a chair and hoped for the best.

A second later, the tooth was out. A new crown was hammered out in the metal workshop until it fitted the girl's tooth. The cod liver oil and vitamin tablets she gave in return cured a number of sick and elderly people.

There was one particular affliction which gave the camp doctors an almost insoluble problem, skin and venereal diseases. There was no dermatologist at this time in the camp, no X-ray treatment, and owing to the lack of vitamins in our diet, every variety of skin disease flourished unchecked. In the severe winters, this lack of vitamins caused many cases of scurvy and gingival atrophy. People lost their teeth, their nails became soft, their bodies were covered with sores. On one occasion, my hands, feet and entire body were covered with pustules.

Miklos Csomos could only look on helplessly at these skin diseases. He said that, although they were not in themselves dangerous, they could cause complications. At times the authorities distributed vitamin pills, but three per head was all they could afford. On the advice of our doctors, Miklos and his colleagues, some of us decided to help ourselves as best we could, and replace the deficiency of green vegetables in our diet with pine needles. They were evil tasting, but at least they contained vitamin C. After chewing these for some days, the symptoms of avitaminosis disappeared; and I still have most of my teeth. Only three fell out while I was a prisoner in Russia.

When we were sent out in the autumn and winter to clear the forests, and to fell trees, we would collect these pine needles, eat them and carry them back to our friends in the camp. It was not easy to smuggle anything into the camp, because the guards made us turn out our pockets, and they took away anything they found, imagining, I suppose, that pine needles were weapons.

During the summer, the problem was simpler, because we could eat grass and young leaves.

Many prisoners suffered from venereal diseases, particularly the more ignorant Russians from Central Asia who had taken part in the European War, where they had indulged in orgies of rape, unaware of the necessary precautions. Some had syphilis in its secondary or tertiary stage, with open sores. Usually the disease was only discovered at this point, because the simpletons had not known what was the matter with them, or had been ashamed to report it. They lived for months among us, sharing our bunks, baths, even using the same half-washed underwear.

When they realised what was wrong they might report it, partly to go to hospital, partly to be exempted from work. The treatment they received was very inadequate, as most of the proper medicines were not available, or in short supply. They could only have a few injections, where dozens would have been the proper treatment. This meant that the symptoms disappeared, but the disease persisted. In the later stages, the syphilitic patients were, fortunately, isolated in a special barrack block.

While on the subject of camp hospitals perhaps I should say something about death. Until 1945-50, prisoners who died were buried in unmarked graves, naked (the clothes were of course confiscated). But, later, when the government needed proof that they had treated these masses of slave labour with "humane consideration," and had given them proper hospital treatment, the camp authorities were ordered to bury them decently in graves. In my time, the dead were placed naked in plain wooden coffins filled with straw. Later, they were given some underclothing, a torn shirt or underpants. The graveyard was outside the camp, wherever possible in a wooded or bush-covered area. A piece of board was put above the grave with the prisoner's registration number, but never his name.

Before 1950 there were no autopsies, partly because of the high mortality, partly because of the inhumane attitude adopted towards slave labour. We heard from some of the prison doctors, and the ex-MVD men imprisoned with us, that in those days the corpses were handed over to an MVD detachment, who took them away in a lorry. The burial was performed by the so-called semi-free labourers who lived outside the camp (such a category of half-prisoner, half-freeman then existed). Their orders were to pierce the chest with an iron spike, not only to prevent anyone from being buried alive, but also to prevent anyone from escaping. Later this practice was stopped. Instead, the skull was crushed with a heavy wooden hammer. They also began to disect the bodies, not on account of humanitarian principles, but in order to discover which epidemics were the most virulent in the concentration camps.

10

Forestry and a Punishment Brigade

DECEMBER 1949

In the early winter of 1949 a special kind of visitor arrived to select skilled and experienced workers for the industrial camps. They called themselves "selectors." We called them slave traders.

The prisoners were divided into four categories, and registered according to physical fitness. General Sergienko, the commandant of the Dubrov camp system, addressed us and said that the period of acclimatisation was over. The time for productive work had come.

The period of acclimatisation he referred to had really served his interests, not ours. It had given him and the slave traders time to catalogue the new prisoners according to their reliability, potential danger to the régime, work capacity, and so on. We were also granted this period, I believe, to help us lose the first feeling of vehement hatred from which rebellion is born.

Of the four grades No. 1 was for the fittest prisoners, who were transferred to the mines in other parts of the country. Grade 2 was for men who were strong enough to do prolonged heavy work. Most of the men in these first two categories were young, under thirty, some under twenty. Grade 3 consisted of men fit only for light work; while Grade 4 consisted of the very old and invalid, unfit for any work.

My physical condition was poor and I was placed

118

in Grade 3. Nevertheless, anyone who had the use of his arms and legs was expected to work beyond his physical capabilities. That many prisoners collapsed and died at work from heart failure, or with cerebral hæmorrhage, confirmed this.

At last the day of our departure from Camp 10, 15th December 1949, arrived. Still in the rags I had worn for the last two and a half years, I stood with my companions knee-deep in the snow, surrounded by detachments of MVD men in huge sheepskin coats, fur caps and heavy felt boots. The Russian political police, like their fellows in Germany, the Gestapo, were granted all the creature comforts; they were better clothed than the Soviet Regular Army itself. The temperature was thirty-five degrees below zero centigrade, but before climbing into the open wagons, we had to stand for over an hour while our personal data were checked for the hundredth time. Frost-bite took its toll that morning, and some of my fellow-prisoners went to hospital when we arrived at our destination.

The MVD guards had several Alsatian dogs, and they amused themselves while we waited by letting these animals loose among us, encouraging them to snap. This was a part of deliberate policy to intimidate us.

We were then taken to Camp 11, which housed the general staff and central administration for the entire Dubrov camp area. It was only twenty-five miles away, but we travelled by wagon for over two hours and finished the journey on foot.

The area around the new camp included the first Russian provincial settlement I had ever seen. One might, I suppose, have called it a town, but it was unlike any town I have ever known in Europe. Only in the illustrations of Fennimore Cooper's Red Indian stories, which I read as a child, have I seen such a collection of primitive log huts and neglected buildings built of clap-board.

We were now in the centre of a large timber-producing region, surrounded by marshes and huge forests, containing oak, beech, and birch trees, many of them hundreds of years old. The birches were enormous, not the variety we had known in Europe. Two men could barely have put their arms around the trunk and touched the tips of their fingers.

We marched through this picturesque little wooden settlement, in which only the military barracks and the administration buildings appeared to be built of brick. The one other piece of solid building was the radio tower, for no expense is spared in Russia over anything connected with "security." All these buildings, including a large industrial plant extending over several square miles, were surrounded by barbed wire and high palisades.

We marched to the factory where we were received by a posse of MVD men who immediately searched us from top to toe. Our personal data were again checked, an administrative procedure invariably accompanying you whenever you move in Russia. I must confess that on this occasion I was surprised at their efficiency; they had not lost any of my documents.

We were then escorted to our barrack block. For lack of space, I was put with the Estonian group into the *karker*, which was larger than the one in Camp 10.*
There were many young people and workers in this camp,

*These *karkers* were of different kinds. In newly built camps they were not underground as in our camp; some were even heated. There was a slight improvement too in this stock camp punishment in later years, especially after the death of Stalin and Beria. It may have been the result of international protest, or perhaps on account of the adoption of more humanitarian ways. But the improvement was so slight as to make very little difference to our lives.

and therefore more opportunity for what was called "sabotage," which accounted for a larger *karker*.

We were kept in quarantine for about a week, during which we met the brigadiers, the foremen and camp administrators, a veritable army of boot-lickers, who bullied us interminably. We seemed to have landed in a new unknown, where the ruthlessness of our slavery would be even worse than before, to be gradually sliding lower and lower down the slope of misfortune.

No sooner had we settled in than I began to suffer for the consequences of my behaviour in Camp 10, when I had retaliated against the brigadier. This brigadier had unfortunately been transferred with us to Camp 11, and he now told his new colleagues about me. Two of my friends overheard him describing me to the man called Rogatshev, one of the most brutal brigadiers in the camp. He told him not only that I had "attacked" him, but that I was a "dangerous fascist," who had murdered quantities of good Russian and European democrats.

Rogatshev evidently intended to show us who he was, for he called me out of the ranks by name the next morning and began cursing me as a "fascist beast and anti-social element." My brigade became most apprehensive at this outburst, but my friend, the tough young Lett, Harry Anderson, spoke up in Russian and told Rogatshev to take care because I was well liked and respected; I was not a fascist. "Rupert is very weak," he said. "He should be given light work. The least you can do is to show him some humanity . . ." I was particularly grateful for this defence because I could not speak Russian myself.

But the brigadier only began cursing louder, accusing Harry of being a fascist too. "It's lucky for you that you've only got one leg, or we'd make short work of you!"

Harry again answered back, telling the brigadier that if he went on like this, he would not remain alive for long; we had powerful friends in the camp, he said, referring to the bandits. This certainly sobered up Rogatshev, for he stopped cursing, but I later heard him muttering he would make an example of us. The "example," as I soon discovered, was to be me.

That evening, I was led to the stock-room where, with a number of old men, I was given warm clothing. I suspected what this meant, a punishment night shift in the open with a temperature forty degrees below zero.

When our companions had gone to bed, we were taken out to one of the railway sidings and told to unload tree-trunks, oak, beech and birch, eighteen feet long, two to four feet in diameter. This kind of work was normally done by the fittest younger prisoners, and then only by day. But we were all ill and one of the old Ukrainians was over seventy. There were eighty of us to unload thirty wagons. We worked from eight o'clock at night until seven in the morning, and we had to unload by hand, as there were no cranes.

Within an hour, two men had broken their arms and another his ribs. One of the old men slipped when a huge trunk rolled towards him, and he failed to jump aside in time. It went right over him crushing his chest: he died almost immediately. An old Ukrianian got down on his knees beside him in the snow, crossed himself and began praying aloud. The brigadier and his assistants ran up and began kicking the kneeling man, ordering him to get up.

We continued working like this, and often during that night I heard the old men crying, "*Bozhe Moi! Bozhe Moi!*" (Oh God! Oh God!) The younger prisoners were filled with such pity that we forgot our own sufferings, and went over to help them. Only at midnight were we allowed a few minutes rest, in the locomotive shed; and when we came out we were greeted by a snowstorm. At the end of this night's work our ears, noses and hands had turned white with frostbite.

The next morning the bell sounded for the *proverka*, and although we had worked all night, we had to attend it in the snow, standing about for over an hour, while lists were consulted and numbers checked. The memory of that first month in Camp 11 will remain with me for ever. I still shudder at it.

This punishment brigade in which I worked for three months killed fifteen of its eighty members. Some died of accidents, some of pleurisy, and some of heart failure. They were given no medical aid, but even if there had been any, it could hardly have saved such old people in these conditions. Fortunately groups of younger prisoners arrived in February and took over the work.

Timber production was one of the most important industries in the region, and it must have become obvious to the camp authorities that the old and the sick were incapable of handling such heavy material. Thus, this first terrible period drew to a close.

After two or three more relatively heavy jobs—in the lumber mill, breaking up the ice-bound ground, laying the foundations of new houses—I found myself, thanks again to Harry Anderson, working beside him in the carpenters' shop. This one-legged ex-S.S. Sergeant (he had been forced into the Latvian S.S. by the Germans) seemed to have a certain influence in the camp, even with the authorities. The work was strenuous, but it was at least indoors.

It was in the carpenters' shop that I was introduced to the infamous Communist norm system. The obligatory minimum, the so-called norm, was determined by the factory management, twenty to twenty-five per cent higher than in civilian factories. When I started work in the carpenters' shop, the daily norm for one worker was the upholstering of fifteen chairs. We received the frames, into which we fitted the square upholstered pieces for the seat, and oblong ones for the back. Everything was done by hand, and we boiled our own glue. A few weeks after I arrived, the norm was raised to twenty chairs a day. At the end of the third month, it went up to thirty-five. This was no longer work, but acrobatics.

The logic which dictated these increased norms was most ingenious. Any output above the norm was rewarded with extra food rations. Those who achieved over a hundred and ten per cent received an extra fifty grammes of mush in the evening. Those who produced over a hundred and twenty per cent, received two hundred grammes of mush and twenty grammes of extra bread—and so on.

It was understandable that some prisoners, particularly the younger ones who were always hungry, tried to produce more and more chairs. In vain, we explained to them that this over-production required more energy, which could not be replaced by the relatively small quantities of extra food. Nor did they listen when we said that they should not serve the Soviet Union so well. Their empty stomachs robbed these simpletons of their reasoning.

Faced with this avalanche of chairs, the camp administration took the obvious course. "All right," they said, "if you can produce chairs so easily, we'll raise the norm by thirty per cent. You have obviously been idling. This is nearer your true figure."

Thus, the achievement of the few became the rule for the many. This was particularly hard on the older prisoners, who could not keep up with the others. They knew that if they lagged behind, they would be transferred to work outside, felling trees, loading and unloading wagons. To avoid this, some of them worked till they dropped.

Thus the authorities had at their disposal means for compelling prisoners to exert superhuman energy. For if this still did not do the trick, the "idle ones" were put in the cold *karker* in their underwear. Here, sometimes, these wretched men had to punch and beat one another, simply to keep their circulation going. Many died here.

It will be appreciated that I had every reason for working hard at my chairs, struggling against this nightmarish arithmetical progression. The manager of our carpenters' workshop was an exceptionally disagreeable woman, who had graduated in the propaganda department, and had been for some time Party Secretary in the local village. Many of the factory managers, the so-called free Russians, were zealous party women who were often more ruthless than the men. This woman drove us like a Fury, not allowing us to exchange so much as a whisper with our neighbours while we worked. She was a norm maniac, in love with expanding percentages.

This hawk-faced female one day went too far. An old Estonian, whom she was reprimanding, picked up the chair he was working on and hit her over the head with it: he did a long spell in the icy *karker* for his action.*

*This courageous old man had once been a *Waldbruder*, one of the partisans of the Estonian woods. When he and his partisan comrades had been finally cornered, he had shot down two MVD officers, and then fled with his machine-gun to a nearby village. Here he waited until all the MVD personnel were at dinner, in their H.Q. that evening; he then entered the mess and coolly fired several bursts at them as they sat at their meal, killing some fifteen before he was captured. He had the luck—if you can call it luck— that at the time the death sentence had been abolished in the Soviet Union.

There was much enmity in this camp between the various national groups, constant fights between Russians and Turks, Poles and Ukrainians, the bandits and the Caucasians. While I was there, three men were stabbed, and one had his head almost cut off. An old White Russian refused to hand over his *mahorka* cigarette to a young Caucasian bandit; so the bandit simply picked up an axe which was being used in the working brigade and tried to decapitate him. I once noticed in the workshop that a group of young prisoners were surreptitiously sharpening knives during the lunch break. When I asked why they were doing this, they replied that the knives had been ordered by the bandits and would be smuggled out to them in the food. Somehow the bandits always seemed to be able to get hold of weapons.

Camp 11 had 1,200 workers in the factory, and 320 administrators, of whom about eighty were free Russians; the other administrators were prisoners selected for their knowledge of book-keeping. Each workshop had its head and assistant book-keepers, working under so many controls, checks and counter-checks that it was surprising anything was produced at all. This inefficiency was redeemed by increased norms, by taking every risk and ignoring all safety precautions. Human life was cheap, and new slaves could always be found if one of them was killed in a factory accident.

Most of the equipment had been confiscated as war reparations from Western countries where the Russian Army had fought. Some of it was modern, but the camp authorities did not know how to use it. The furniture factory where I worked was equipped with good rotary saws and planing machines, but there were no trained operators. After three days' training, prisoners were expected to use equipment which, in the West, would have required at least three weeks' apprenticeship. The older, less well nourished prisoners grew tired at work, and lost their power of concentration; their reflexes were slow, and they could not use the circular saw properly. I often saw old men running off to the first aid station their fingers or hands dripping with blood.

The circular saws revolved at three thousand revolutions a minute, but there was no automatic brake or splinter screen. Sometimes, a piece of oak would split, and a splinter would be shot off with the force of a bullet. In one case, the splinter took half the back of the man's head away, and then went on to penetrate a wooden wall behind. In the second, the tooth of a circular saw broke off, and hit the man in the forehead, coming out through the back of his head. We hardly realised what had happened: he suddenly collapsed, dead, spattering everyone with blood.

The camp had a power station which produced electricity not only for the camp, but for the entire MVD village outside. It had been built in 1923 and was very primitive. The electric cables had been laid without safety precautions, so that workers were continually getting electric shocks, some of them fatal.

In certain woodwork shops, central heating had been installed, not for the benefit of the workers, but because heat was necessary for drying and varnishing the wood. The steam was led by underground pipes to the workshops from the power plant, containing a giant boiler. These pipes were also poorly laid and there were constant explosions, and people were always being scalded.

I continued working in the carpenters' shop until May, when I was summoned one morning before the *oper*, the amp MVD officer.* As I suspected, this was in onnection with the woman who managed the chair-naking. She had ordered me to produce five additional hairs a day, which meant another two hours work daily. had therefore asked her what the norm was. "I want o know," I said, "because you are entitled to ask me to ulfil the norm. But no more."

She went scarlet with rage and said she would show me vho was master. The *oper* told me that as a result of her omplaint and my earlier trouble with the brigadier, I was o be transferred to Brigade 72, the most notorious of the unitive brigades.

Members of Brigade 72 lived in a special barrack block vhich they were forbidden to leave, and they were not llowed to talk to the other prisoners. Their place of vork was far removed from those of the others, and they vere supervised by a special detachment of soldiers, rom whom they even had to ask permission to go to the atrine. In spite of this, I managed to communicate by igns and messages with Antonos Bruzhas who would vave to me as I went to work. "Keep smiling!" I emember him shouting. "We'll soon get together gain somehow." He even managed to smuggle me some obacco. The Englishman, Alec Peters, was also in this Brigade. We were known as the "two bloody British pies".

My task in this brigade was to dig up large tree stumps vith their roots, and carry them to the saw-mill across he marshes. The camp was built on marshland, so that ve sank into the peat at every step under the weight of hese stumps. There were many accidents; the stumps,

*These summonings were not unusual for prisoners whom he authorities considered politically dangerous. By frequent questioning, they hoped to involve more and more of our friends n the West.

some of which weighed half a ton, rolled on to the prisoners, crushing them. During my first week of this work, fifteen prisoners had to be taken to hospital.

My group was not very adept and one morning we dropped our tree which rolled directly towards me, knocking me down and striking the back of my head. I was lucky not to have had my head crushed. This happened at noon in midsummer, when we were working in the burning sun. Blood appeared before my eyes. My nose began to bleed, and when I tried to rise, I stumbled and lost consciousness.

When I recovered, I had lost all muscular power; I could not move a leg or arm and lay there half conscious, blinded in one eye. My Ukrainian fellow workers immediately ran to the guards, who sent for a *feldsher*. The *feldsher* examined me, saw that I was paralysed and could not walk, and said I must be carried to the infirmary. He asked the other prisoners to hoist me on to his back, and he then carried me himself to the guard hut five hundred yards away. Here I fainted again.

He telephoned to the administration that I should be transferred from the labour camp to the dwelling camp. It took half an hour to obtain this permission, while he tried repeatedly to revive me. Each time that I regained consciousness, I fainted again and I thought I was going to die. He then lifted me on to his back, and carried me another half mile. He certainly saved my life that morning, and he too collapsed from the heat when he reached the infirmary.

For two days, I remained unconscious, and when I recovered I found that my right side was paralysed; I could move neither my arm nor leg. My lips were drawn to the right, and when I tried to drink water it trickled out of the corner of my mouth. The doctor in charge of my case was very different from the *feldsher*.

He said I was shamming, and began scratching and cutting the skin on the sole of my right foot until it bled, to test me for a reflex action.

I remained in the infirmary for three weeks, until I could move my limbs a little. But it was another two months before I could stand, and then only with crutches, because my right leg seemed to have lost the use of its muscles. Dr. Suba, a Hungarian physician friend, advised me to pretend I was paralysed. "If you show you can move your right side at all," he said, "they'll send you back to the Punitive Brigade, as 'cured.' That blow caused bleeding under your skull and you've had cerebral hæmorrhage. You'll die if you go back to work."

He gave me a pen-knife and recommended me, in order to foil the Russian doctor, to scratch the soles of my feet and the skin of my belly regularly until they bled. I carefully practiced not wincing, and succeded in misleading the doctor, who at last pronounced me as Grade 4. I was therefore transferred to Camp 14.

I I

In a Factory

On arrival in Camp 14 I was immediately given another medical examination. The Russian doctor here was a kind of Devil's Advocate in reverse, interested only in the good or healthy side of a prisoner's physique. He wanted to upgrade me; but the chief physician, who had been disabled in the war, took one look at me and told him not to waste time. He endorsed my three months' period in Grade 4.

Although this absolved me from productive work, I still had plenty to do in the routine cleaning of the camp, in the kitchens, raking and cleaning the sand strip between the wire fences, cleaning the palisades. Two brigades of cripples were employed all day, fetching water from the well for the kitchen and the bakery. But these three months at least gave me a respite, a chance to take part in some sort of social life, even to develop my interests. I had always wanted to improve my English, and here I had the opportunity to do so.

I made friends with some elderly Russian prisoners who had lived for years in Shanghai and who spoke excellent English. They had unwisely returned to Russia in the twenties, hoping to find the "socialist paradise". The problem was to obtain writing materials. At first we wrote in the sand, with a stick or with our fingers, ten or twelve words which we would learn by heart. Later, we wrote with a piece of coal on wooden slates

made from the bark of trees. Finally, we acquired from
the KVC, the Camp Cultural Centre (such a place really
existed in Camp 14!) one or two small stubs of pencil.
Prisoners would steal them or barter them for a piece of
bread. About twenty of us would then share one small
stub. We hid these with our writings in cracks under
the barrack floors, or under clumps of grass which we dug
up with our hands. We were later able to use the paper
which the book-keepers used for writing in their offices.
No white paper was available in Russia; all account
books were made of packing paper.

Continuing these intellectual pursuits, we formed little
groups, each specialising in its own particular subject.
I gave lectures to Rumanians and Balts on Central
European history, law, economics, and literature. Although our knowledge of English was limited, the
lingua franca was English. It was amusing to listen to a
provincial Hungarian talking English to an Estonian
gardener, or a Latvian sailor discussing Byron in English
with a Polish shoemaker. One of our friends, a Rumanian
journalist, had been the Bucharest correspondent of the
Daily Mail before the war. He had a good memory,
and when we later managed to steal packing paper from
the book-keeping offices, he would write out excerpts
from English novels or short stories he had read. I
remember with pleasure Somerset Maugham's *The Letter*,
a part of which he could recite by heart. He would also
write essays in English about the flora and fauna of his
own country, particularly in the Danube delta. He
described his beautiful country so graphically that his
English essays were among our most treasured possessions; they went from hand to hand, and everyone learned
a part. I also made friends with a Lithuanian poet,
Mishkinis. Although he had never been in England,
he spoke excellent English, and he gave a series of

lectures on Byron and Keats. Mishkinis was one of the best known poets of his country.

All this was very pleasant, but it was also dangerous. Discovery meant being sentenced to several days in the *karker*, or expelled from the tailoring factory and put on outdoor work.

After three months, I was upgraded to Grade 3, and put to work again. I had hoped to get into a factory, because it was mid-winter, but there were too many old men who had to be given the inside jobs, and I was put in a brigade erecting new houses and repairing old ones. It was unwise to build these new houses in winter in the Dubrov marshland, because when the summer came the heat thawed and softened the frozen soil, and the buildings toppled over. I remember seeing small bridges which we had built in winter, become lopsided in the warm weather. And yet we were made to build continually, because a house lasts only five years in this climate; it then rots and has to be replaced. We used oak or beech stakes for foundations; we charred them first, then sunk them in the soil as piles.

While repairing buildings outside the camp, I had an opportunity of seeing the home life of the officials and officers of the MVD. They were the privileged class of Russia, and one might have expected their houses to possess at least the bourgeois amenities. But most of the interiors I saw revealed nothing but dirt, stench and incredible poverty. Their owners had no proper furniture and they sat on boxes. Sometimes they slept on a wooden or iron camp bed; more often, the beds were formed by two wooden trestles, joined by a plank covered with a blanket. There were no carpets or linoleum, and the floors were never swept. Pots and pans did not exist, and the cooking was done in tins. Instead of glasses they used aluminium or earthenware mugs. Later, when they heard there was an Austrian turner in the camp, they obtained wooden mugs from him. They spat on the floor, and in the winter, if they felt it was too cold to go to the latrine, they ripped up a floorboard and relieved themselves in their own rooms. In summer the stench was unbearable. We prisoners hated them most for this; we had to clear it up. If there were plenty of fleas and bed bugs in our prison quarters, I now found that there were more in the houses of the officials and free Russians who lived outside. In fact, one of the MVD officers told me he would prefer to live with us in the camp—because it was so clean!

After several unsuccessful attempts at obtaining a factory job, I was lucky in the spring. I entered the clothing factory thanks to one of the section managers, a Hungarian tailor, who asked for me although he knew I was untrained. His staff was almost exclusively European, because the work required some intelligence and accuracy. The norm was, as usual, ridiculously high, but I was delighted to see how my colleagues ingeniously overcame this. Sometimes the factory would stop work for days, even weeks, because of a lack of raw materials or spare parts—which they generally engineered themselves.

In Socialist planning on a nation-wide scale, the lack of one type of button, or a hook, or a broken needle, which cannot be replaced, brings production to a standstill. On one occasion, the neighbouring furniture factory ran out of glue, and it stopped work for ten days. Another time, a small wooden nail caused a standstill for a day. The sewing machines were attached to a single transmission belt, so that if this was out of order all the machines stopped. We learned various ways of damaging this belt, and we poured sand into the lubricating oil. To see some of the excellent British diesel engines, which had been taken in Czechoslovakia as reparation at the end of the war, break down as a result of our own sabotage was heartrending. But we overcame our scruples, and generally had at least one machine out of action.

Another difficulty which we aggravated, but which the authorities really brought on themselves, was lack of stock, woollen stuff, linings, cotton wool, padding, etc. I heard later from a Russian textile expert that it was a deliberate part of Soviet industrial policy not to keep stock. To pile up raw material, more at least than was needed for two or three days' work, was "sabotage"—because "raw material was lying unused"! We used about fifteen thousand yards of this wool lining every day in the tailor's shop, and it arrived, or was supposed to arrive, daily. It was still damp when it arrived, having just been taken off the looms; it had not dried properly, and as it dried in our shop, it shrank. For fifteen thousand yards, the shrinkage was considerable; this was most convenient, because anything stolen could be attributed to "shrinkage." Everyone stole the lining—the prisoners, the free workers, the guards, the managers. Yet, at the half-yearly stocktaking, the vast quantity of missing material was always listed as "shrunken stock." Russian engineers and business-men told me that wherever political prisoners were employed in factories it was the same; there was always sabotage and pilfering of this kind.

The fundamental reason for all these troubles was that the industrial system was rotten. The Soviet Union was over-centralised, economically as well as politically. Everything was planned and calculated at headquarters thousands of miles away; everything arrived late, because communications were still poor, and centralised planning demands above all good communications. Not until

Khrushchev came to power was any attempt made to remedy this. An intelligent Russian industrial expert, now a prisoner, explained all this to me one evening.

"But," I argued, "the Russian forces looted half Europe. They dismantled thousands of factories and stole some first-class machinery. I saw it myself. At the Egyesult Izzo factory in Budapest, for instance."

"Yes," he said, "we dismantled and took away everything we could lay hands on, it is true. But we have not really profited from it. What did not fall to pieces on the way to Russia, was ruined later. The distribution of all the machinery taken after the war was not organised. The greater part of it was left in the open, exposed to snow and frost, to rust and disintegrate."

A teacher who came from the Carpathian regions told me about a modern paper mill which had been dismantled in this way by the Russians in Austria, and its machinery transported through Hungary as far as Raho in the Carpathian mountains. He said he had seen these machines thrown out on to a siding in Raho. That was in 1945. He was then kidnapped, and sentenced to three years' imprisonment in Russia for some imaginary crime. When the sentence was over, and he was returning through Raho in 1948, he saw the same machinery, now rusty, *still scattered in exactly the same position along the railway line.*

The tailor's factory was an excellent advertisement for American Singer sewing machines, because some of them here were 1920 models. Old and battered as they were, they still ran. How they ran! When our norms went up, the sewing machines had to work harder too. The revolutions are, I believe, not supposed to exceed fifteen to eighteen hundred a minute. But our Singer sewing machines ran at two thousand five hundred, or even three thousand revolutions a minute. The needles jumped frenziedly up and down, and sometimes the material under them began to steam.

While working here, I met a Russian with the Anglicised name of James Bragin, who had been educated at Edinburgh University. His admiration for Britain was boundless, and he had deliberately changed his name so that it could be pronounced in an English way. When he heard that I had worked for the British in Vienna, he became ecstatic and would hardly speak to anyone else. Poor fellow, it was his Anglo-mania which had landed him in jail.

Before the war he had worked in Archangel with a firm exporting timber, which had enabled him to keep up his connections with England. When the war came, he was sent to the Caucasus, and it was here that he saw Mrs. Churchill when she visited Russia on behalf of the Red Cross in 1943. When her car passed along the road surrounded by a jubilant crowd, he became immensely excited and shouted, "How glad we are that you have come, Madam! How grateful we are to you British! Welcome to our country!"

Although his countrymen were surprised that his English was so good, Britain was then an ally, and no one could take exception to this—officially. But the authorities were vigilant; they had noted his words. After the war he was interrogated. What were his British connections? He told me he had often spoken to friends in private about his love of Great Britain. He later discovered that almost every word he had said had been recorded. This, together with his friendly salutation to Mrs. Churchill, was enough to brand him as a "saboteur disseminating enemy propaganda." He had been sentenced to fifteen years' hard labour.

We became very intimate, almost like father and son (he was aged sixty-eight), a friendship which continued until his death in 1953, when his case was being reinvestigated. He was granted an amnesty, but the poor man died two weeks before he was freed. He never saw his wife and children again.

12

On the Land

The work in the tailors' shop was the least disagreeable that I had to do during my imprisonment. I did it as well as my technical ignorance would allow, but I was now neither fit enough, nor quick enough, to satisfy the ever-increasing demands of the norm maniacs. My paralysis returned partially at one point. They rejected me, and I was sent to work on the land.

This might have been unpleasant, but for two reasons I did not regret the change. The first was that I have had a lifelong love of the country, and I shall never forget the beauty of the Russian landscape.

We would start out from camp at dawn when a silvery mist still hung over the trees. The sky gradually turned yellow and little breezes carried with them the smell of hay. Then one would catch the first faint voices of the forest which was full of wild life. Several times I found the traces of bears and we frequently came upon elk, wolves and wild boar, not to mention the smaller animals and the birds. There were eagles, ravens, capercaillie, and black-cock, which the Russian prisoners somehow managed to trap. I recall shafts of silver light above the marshes and the movement of wild geese high overhead, and longing for my shot-gun.

I often discussed the richness of the wild life and the opportunities for sport with a German in our brigade,

Dr. Walter Schmidt.* We agreed that this was one of the most beautiful countries in the world.

"I bet you that one day," he laughed, "the present system will be swept away and we shall be able to come back with our shot-guns and our fishing rods."

The rivers teemed with fish. During the mid-day break we would try catching them in the baskets we used for our work. Some of the Russians would fashion traps out of the reeds and others could even catch the fish in their bare hands, eating them raw with salt. Once, we saw a battle between an otter and a giant pike amidst so much splashing that we thought someone must have fallen into the river.

But apart from these distractions I was fascinated, while working on the land, to see the *kolkhoz*† system in action. I had some theoretical knowledge of *kolkhozes* from the propaganda films which had been shown once a month, in the dining hall. In one of these, I had seen the *kolkhoz* to which the wife and son of President Roosevelt were taken. Judging from their remarks, the Americans were favourably impressed.

There are, of course, many well-organised collective farms in Russia, especially near the railway lines; but they were only a fraction of the great *kolkhoz* system extending throughout the Soviet Union. Certain Russian agriculture experts who were our fellow prisoners were much amused by these films. "We Russians have always known how to cheat the world," they said. "When will the world wake up to reality? If it was a Potemkin‡

*He is now a West German diplomat in Chile.

†Collective farm.

‡Potemkin, Grigory Aleksandrovich (1739-1791) a favourite of Catherine II, on whom she lavished many honours. He concealed the weak points of the régime, and is celebrated chiefly for his "Potemkin villages," which were specially built to impress foreigners

Russia in the time of Catherine the Great, it is even more a Potemkin Russia to-day. Only on a greater scale. Those distinguished American visitors are unaware that our livestock was reduced by this *kolkhoz* system to ten per cent of what it was in 1914."

They were right. The foreigner who visits these farms has not the slightest idea of what is happening in Russian agriculture. He goes to the show-places which are full of beautiful smiling maidens in national costumes, model housing estates, farm hospitals, new communal cinemas and cultural amenities. If he were to dig a little deeper into Russia, he would be most surprised at the contrast between the real *kolkhozes* and these.

The *sorkhoz* or State farm (not the *kolkhoz*), which deals scientifically with husbandry and agricultural improvements, and with the production of high grade quality crops, is relatively well run. It is neither better nor worse than most European farms. But it is an experimental State farm, and there are few of them. The ordinary *kolkhoz* which produces, in its thousands, food for the nation, not only in agriculture, but in stock breeding, fishing, even in hunting, is quite a different matter.

My Russian and Ukrainian farming friends told me that the *kolkhoz* I worked in was worth examining closely, because it was typical, repeated throughout the country, over millions of square miles. A *kolkhoz* had approximately a thousand acres* and was worked by three hundred and fifty peasants, which was ten times as many

---

with the prosperity of rural Russia. They were built for the occasion, in cheap but showy materials and lasted only a short time.

*In the early 1950's the small collectives underwent a process of amalgamation, to make larger units of between 5,000 and 20,000 acres.

as were necessary, or could be supported by the land. It had three cows and thirty goats, all of them small, lean and neglected. Nor were the horses much better— spavined and broken-backed, with disproportionately large heads; they looked as if they needed crutches. The work was done almost exclusively by human beings, even the harrow being drawn by men or women, because there were no tractors, and the horses were unfit. Human beings ploughed, hoed, sowed, dug—about fifty of them working in a line with their spades. Most of them were women or children, or men over sixty (the younger ones were needed in the factories).

In theory, tractor stations had been installed all over the province; but the machines were evidently needed elsewhere, or were out of order, for we never saw them. The few which we were lent were almost unusable, because no one knew how to maintain them. Their lubricating oil had been stolen by the peasants and sold on the black market.

It was the same with livestock. The cows and horses were starving, because the fodder had been eaten by the peasants. They also stole, or ate, the seeds they were supposed to sow. In the spring, they prepared, or seemed to be preparing, the soil for sowing. But when autumn and harvest-time arrived, and everyone expected a crop, nothing appeared. If the culprit was discovered, he would be given ten years for "sabotage." But this did not make "a blade grow where no blade was."

Living conditions for the peasants were correspond-ingly wretched. The cottages, or hovels, were dirty and smelly, overrun with mobs of bare-footed, half-naked children in rags, who had never drunk the milk of the cow in their lives. They might occasionally have a little goats' milk; but few peasants could afford a goat. Child mortality was enormous; but if these infants had not died in such quantities, the country would have been over-populated. Nearly all the women were pregnant in the spring, like their cows.

These particular *kolkhozniks* belonged to the Mordvin nation of forest dwellers, a forgotten, struggling little community which I have already described. They had now been reduced by forced migration to a fraction of their original size, but they were trying to preserve their nationality and traditions as best they could. Their children often came to the camp, or to our working parties, with water, asking if they might have some bread in return. We could not refuse, and if we had any we gave it to them.

A Mordvin peasant family possessed one pair of shoes, and one overcoat. Whoever went out in the open in the winter—whether it was the father, mother or son—put them on. Even the wives of the MVD officials who were living in the neighbourhood wore the military greatcoats of their husbands. Shoes were so expensive and scarce that no peasant possessed a pair. Instead, the *kolkhozniks* wore slippers made out of the inner bark of trees. The foot was first wrapped in rags, then came the wooden slipper, and the rags were finally wound round the leg and tied on with string. There was a workshop in the camp which produced these slippers, boiling the bark first to soften it. They were also worn by some of my fellow-prisoners.

The *kolkhozes* often took part in production competitions, hoping to obtain a premium; but the rewards for which the peasants risked their lives were generally illusory. They challenged one another, committing themselves to produce so much grain, tomatoes, or carrots, above the previous year's production. They sent enthusiastic telegrams to Stalin, and the newspaper *Pravda*, and received equally effusive replies, which they quoted to everyone. But how could they know what the harvest would produce? Everything depended, first on the weather, secondly on a sound economy. The first was God-given, the second did not exist.

This form of "Socialist" competition is universal throughout the Soviet Union, not only for groups but also for individuals, the Stakhanovite or new Soviet hero. The Stakhanovite was the man or woman who surpassed the limits of human endeavour in any given field of production, agricultural or industrial. Exceptional Stakhanovites were put on the train and sent to meet the great Red Tsar Stalin in Moscow, for handshakes and back-slapping.

The glamour and glory which surrounded these heroes seldom lasted long. Sooner or later, the human machine could not maintain such high standards, and it broke down. The law of nature would not allow the misuse of the human body. In a year or two the Stakhanovite had become a forgotten little man—sometimes even, in his desire to achieve the exaggerated norm, a "saboteur."

These competitions also took place in our prison camps, although we were not allowed to use the sacred word Stakhanovites. Our work maniacs were known as "recordists."

13

The "Saints"

I have often been asked what enabled people to remain sane and survive in these concentration camps. Naturally, physique was of tremendous importance. The ill and the old stood little chance of resisting the intense cold and the overwork to which they were driven. Apart from this, education was a great advantage for it at least gave one mental resources to fall back on. Men like Csomos and Bruzhas were saved by a sense of humour. But above all, as I found myself, it was a faith of some kind which kept people human.

Outstanding in the camps were the priests of the various denominations, and the other prisoners will always remember how much they did. Their wisdom and philosophical calm in the midst of so much unhappiness and suffering gave us the necessary courage and spiritual force to go on. They set aside their own tragedies—the memories of the families which they, too, had had to leave behind—to help the rest of us. They somehow organised prayers, services, and occasionally choir singing, and constantly diverted our minds I remember particularly when I made my first confession in prison. It was to an old Ukrainian Uniat priest in the corner of an overcrowded cell in Lvov. He gave me absolution and told me to put my faith and trust in God, because only thus would I have the moral strength to face the future.

The most distinguished of the priests I met in the

camps was Slipei, the Metropolitan Archbishop of Lvov, head of the Uniat church which observes Greek Rites but recognises the Pope. (Its members are mostly Ukrainians, but it also includes Rumanians and Hungarians.) The arrival of this bishop gave fresh hope to the prisoners, and we were much in need of consolation. A man of his moral stature provided it. He was no longer young, having spent many years in Russian captivity. The official Russian Church authorities, the new Orthodox Church recreated by Stalin (their church did not recognise the authority of the Pope) had done their best to persuade him to join their ranks, but found him unyielding. However, they had approached his subordinates and had, in some cases, been successful.

The Achilles' heel of most of these Uniat priests was their families. To support their wives and children some of them yielded, knowing that otherwise they would be sent to prison and their families would starve. The majority refused to give up their faith, thereby suffering the same fate as their leader. But the others, who yielded to the Communist demands, later received their rewards at the hands of the people. The partisan movement, headed by the Ukrainians, was merciless to apostates, and many of these renegade priests were assassinated.

The Roman Catholic priests were luckier than the Uniats because they were unmarried; they could not be blackmailed through their families. One of these, a Hungarian Benedictine, Tibor Meszaros, who had been master of ceremonies to Cardinal Mindszenty in Hungary, used to say Mass daily, and prisoners from all over the camp would attend; we would also make our confessions to him. Even the bandits respected him. If they happened to be in the room at the time they would sit quietly and not disturb the service. Sometimes, they even undertook to stand guard at the door, and warn us when the authorities were approaching.

Religious services were, of course, strictly forbidden; even to say one's prayers was regarded as a demonstration against the Communist system. The services were therefore clandestine. The Catholic priests would often say Mass in the dark at night, in their own bunks, lying or half-kneeling.*

Another Catholic priest who made a great impression on us was an Italian Jesuit, Father Leoni. He had been sent by the Holy See to Odessa towards the end of the war, when Russia and the West were allied. When the alliance broke up, he was arrested as a spy and sentenced to twenty-five years' imprisonment. He had been here ten years, and had somehow always managed to give religious instruction and even perform missionary work. His gentle smiling face concealed great strength of character, and gave us immense support. On one occasion he revealed his courage in an unforgettable way.

The authorities had impertinently introduced the "Dove of Peace" campaign into the camp. It was not enough that the Soviet Government should force their own hundred and eighty millions to sign the "Peace Movement" manifesto; they also required the signatures of their prisoners.

In one of the corners of our dining barracks a large stage had been erected, with a table on which lay the manifesto. Behind the table stood the camp commandant, ten MVD officials and other members of the administrative staff. We prisoners were marched in, and the commandant made a speech in which he said that the Soviet Union had introduced many improvements for

*It was a very moving moment for me when, in London in 1959, I met Father Tibor Meszaros again and he asked me if I would take orders. He is now in Hungary.

the prisoners in the last few years. He wanted us to show our loyalty and gratitude by signing the book on the table before him. We would thus help the Soviet Union to achieve peace throughout the world. He asked us to step forward separately and sign.

The first prisoner was about to step forward, when a loud voice at the back shouted in perfect Russian: "Anyone who puts his name in that book, signs his own death warrant."

For a moment there was silence. "Who said that?" shouted the commandant. We all knew it was Father Leoni, but no one said a word. The camp guards ran up and down at the back in a fruitless search. Then suddenly some of the prisoners began laughing; the laughter turned to cheering, and soon we had all left the barrack room. The officials remained behind alone, with their empty "Peace" book. Father Leoni was never caught or punished for his outburst. (I should add that this incident took place after 1953, that is, in the more humane Khrushchev era.)

The Protestant ministers in our camp were equally courageous. Then there were priests of religions I had not heard of, the so-called Armenian Independent Free Catholic Church, which had flourished in the Caucasus. This religion did not recognise the Pope, but its leaders were in a real sense Christian.

I have spoken of the Mohammedans, who found great solace in their religion. They practised it more openly than any other group, always performing the ritual ablutions. They had a muezzin, a member of the lower clergy, who did his work among them with self-effacing conscientiousness, and nothing could prevent them from obeying his calls to prayer.

The Buddhist religion was represented by two shepherds, mystics who were constantly praying, and going about their religious duties in a calm and dignified way. We did not know their language, and they had some difficulty in expressing their wants in their strange tongue. Other denominations included Nazarenes, Baptists, and various sects which had seceded from the Orthodox Church, whose names were unfamiliar to me. They all held most of their services in the evening, in secret, or early in the morning behind the barracks, so as to give the impression of carrying on an ordinary conversation.

There was one man whose special religion prescribed three days of religious holiday every week. On these days he would not touch tools, or do work of any kind. In spite of every threat, including a spell in the *karker*, he would not yield. Finally, he was sent away to a mental asylum. To the Communists he was, I suppose, a lunatic.

Another religious group whom the Communists probably considered as lunatics were the Russian Quakers. Single-minded and dauntless they had written a letter to Stalin asking him to "return to God and mend his ways," adding that they would forgive him if he did so. This letter must have so surprised the Kremlin authorities that they did nothing about it for several months, warily waiting to see if it was perhaps connected with an assassination plot. When they realised that the Quakers were perfectly sincere in the sentiments they had expressed, they arrested the lot and hurried them off to our camp.

One memorable night towards the end of my imprisonment stands out in my mind. A number of our friends had just left to be repatriated, and a common bond seemed to unite the members of all religions. Not only Catholics and Protestants, but Buddhists and Jews, Orthodox and Jehovah's Witnesses, Baptists and Armenian Independent Free Catholics, all sang the *Te*

Deum together. Although we ourselves were not going home, we rejoiced for our more fortunate friends. An old Greek Orthodox priest said a prayer aloud, and a Protestant minister assisted him. Not even the guards disturbed us that night (and they could have done so for we made no secret of the service). One of them even said, "Pray on! It seems there is still someone above who hears your prayers!" This was an old Communist who had fought in the Lenin period.

I had never known anything quite like it before, nor have I experienced it since, in the free Western world in which I now live—that dozens of people, of different faiths and nationalities should be so united in thanksgiving for the good fortune of others.

14

The Cynics

There was a very different type of prisoner, whom I shall remember as vividly as the priests, the stool-pigeon, to whom I have already briefly referred. At no time was there a shortage of these unpleasant creatures in the camps, some of them, I am sorry to say, Europeans, who should never have sunk so low. I had some unfortunate experiences in the early days when I was still ignorant of camp life, and became a dupe to other Hungarians who apparently wanted to talk about friends at home.

The first of these was a Hungarian Army officer who was most affable, continually trying to win my confidence by telling me about his connections with the camp kitchen (my readers will appreciate by now the attraction of this). Apart from the prospect of food, I was pleased to talk to a new friend, particularly a Hungarian who had, like me, been in the army, and who appeared so civilised and friendly. I accepted the extra food several times. Always, with great subtlety, he then managed to turn the conversation on to my connections with the West.

"I know you are not a British spy," he said, "but you have spent much time in the West. It would be interesting to know how people live there. I have been here in prison so much longer than you that I am starved for information about the West."

He asked me what I had done in Austria, the names of my friends, of all the interesting people I had met in

Vienna while working at the British H.Q. I told him a little, but nothing that could incriminate anyone. I soon became very careful about names. The Russians could easily kidnap people from Austria, or from any of the other countries occupied by their armies, and accuse them of being Western agents, simply because they once knew me.

When he saw my reticence, he became impatient; he began interrupting, asking me to speak about more specific things, less about generalities. Once, when he brought me extra food from the kitchen, I was surprised to see him staring at it hungrily himself. I offered him some.

"No, it's for you," he said. "Go on! You must eat it all."

I asked what he meant by saying I *must* eat it all. Surely he, not the camp authorities, had obtained it for me? When I told my other friends about this, they found it most suspicious. Those whom I trusted implicitly said they had not said anything to me before about him, as he appeared to be my friend; but he was frequently to be seen at night leaving his barrack block, on the pretext of going to the latrine, but in fact visiting the night duty officer in the camp *oper* office. Next time he came with food, I told him I was not hungry.

Another Hungarian of the same kind also claimed to be an army officer, a major (I later discovered he had not even been an n.c.o.). He professed great patriotism, and became so emotional when referring to Hungary that he brought tears to the eyes of some of the younger Hungarians. They were so moved that they were even induced to give him some of their food. By now I had become more experienced and told them to beware of this smooth-tongued man. One day I told him to his face, in front of the younger Hungarians, that I did not trust him. He said nothing and appeared as charming as ever; but I knew he was furious. My suspicions were well founded.

Some days later, I was summoned to the commandant's office, where the political officer asked me severely what I had against this fellow countryman? What was our quarrel? This was extremely unsubtle of him, and I laughed out loud. Who else could have told him of "our quarrel?"

I heard later from a Hungarian army doctor that he had found certain papers which this man had left by an oversight when working in hospital No. 9. Among them was a report on the frame of mind and general morale of the Hungarian prisoners! The doctor confronted the "major" with this document. Although the man generally had a ready answer to everything, he was speechless; he could only stammer, and then he fell on his knees in front of the doctor, and asked him not to tell the other Hungarians about it. The doctor replied that if he ever came across him in the free world he would kill him like a mad dog.

Another "charmer" was a German whose name, Rupner, was so similar to mine that we became involved in a curious incident. He was a former landowner in Galicia, and he would talk so brilliantly, in the sophisticated, *homme du monde* manner, that some of the younger prisoners were mesmerised by him.

One of the Poles told me about Rupner's past. During the German occupation, he had lived in Lvov, where he had made a fortune out of Jews who wanted to escape to Hungary and Rumania. (Although there were anti-Jewish laws in these countries, there were no extermination camps.) Rupner had a large motor van and, in return for cash or jewellery, he would agree to take Jews to the frontier, where friends could help them across. He told them that he had fitted his van with curtains, so that they should not be recognised on the journey. In no circumstances, if they valued their lives, should they open the curtains or look out while he transported them. These curtains prevented them seeing where they were going. After driving in the neighbourhood for an hour or so, he would take them to the headquarters of the local Gestapo in Lvov, and hand them over. These unfortunate Jews were later forced by the Gestapo to write letters to their friends and relations, saying that they had arrived safely in Hungary or Rumania, and recommending them to take the same route. This was a most lucrative traffic for Rupner.

He also ingeniously managed, while working for the Gestapo, to serve in the underground movement against the Germans! Thus, he calculated that whoever won the war, he would be on the winning side. This had evidently not availed him, for here he was with us in prison.

He was finally involved in an escape plot, which almost resulted in his death, but at the hands of the prisoners, not the camp guards. He planned with four other Poles to escape in the snow over the barbed wire by a fire ladder. When the night for the escape came, the other Poles climbed to the top of the ladder as arranged, but Rupner, at the last moment stayed below. These unfortunate men then found themselves suddenly illuminated in the beam of a searchlight on the watch tower. The guards had been waiting for them and they opened fire immediately. Two Poles were killed, and the others were badly wounded. Rupner remained unscathed.

The Polish and Ukrainian prisoners in the camp held a secret "military tribunal" among themselves after this, accusing Rupner of treason. They then solemnly passed sentence of death on him. What occurred then followed the usual pattern. About two weeks later a man wearing a handkerchief around his face broke into Rupner's hut one night while he was asleep and stabbed him. He intended to kill him, but he was disturbed by a passing guard and his attack was not fatal. Rupner was taken to hospital with his throat badly gashed. It was here that our two names, Rupner and Rupert, became confused.

Some days later a camp guard came into my barracks in the middle of the night and asked for me. "Rup . . . Rupp . . . Ruppert . . . ?" he said. He said the camp commandant wanted to see me immediately. I did not like these midnight interrogations, so I woke a friend, an Estonian who spoke Russian, and asked him to accompany me as interpreter. In reality, I wanted a witness.

When we reached the office, the commandant was extremely annoyed; he said he had summoned only one man, not two and he asked which was Rupner. I said my name was Rupert, not Rupner.

" But you are not Rupner? How long have you been here?"

" Three years," I replied.

He realised there had been a mistake and began cursing the guard who had summoned me. We were then dismissed.

When we returned to our barracks we told the Poles and Ukrainians about this. Two of them immediately ran out in the dark to the commandant's office and were just in time to see Rupner arriving, his neck still bandaged. Through the window they watched him talking with the political officer. The conversation lasted an hour and a half.

The Poles and Ukrainians now determined to make another attempt on Rupner's life when he left hospital.

But Rupner was too clever. Somehow, when he recovered, he managed to be transferred to another camp. We heard that he had been sent to Karaganda in Central Asia, far away, where no one knew him.

A less frequent kind of stool-pigeon was the prisoner, often one of our close friends, who was forced by the camp authorities to become an informer, in order to protect his family. In such cases we generally tried to help him in preparing his reports, and we were often able to give the camp authorities false information.

One of the tragedies connected with this, which affected me most closely concerned a Balt friend, a likeable but naïve young man who was suffering from leukaemia, and who found himself in this unpleasant situation. The MVD said that if he did not inform about certain prisoners (I was interested to learn that I was one of them), he would be transferred from his task in the hospital and put, in the depths of winter, on outdoor work. He consulted us about this; we advised him that he should give up his hospital work rather than accept such a shameful proposal.

He returned to the MVD officer and said that, because his fellow prisoners already suspected him of having obtained his hospital job by duplicity, he could not accept the conditions. The MVD officer said he would report to his superiors that the stubbornness of the young Balt came from the anti-Communist education he had received at home, in Latvia; they would recommend that his family should, for the sake of security, be deported to Siberia.

We again discussed the matter carefully, and finally agreed that, because of his family, he should accept the "informing" work. We made the proviso that we should help him in composing his reports. In doing this we were careful not to be too factual, and we made him emphasise the difficulties he encountered in questioning us.

Unfortunately, Harry Anderson, the one-legged Latvian who had been so good to me, decided to use this as an opportunity for paying off old scores with certain MVD officers in Latvia, where he had been arrested. We advised him against this. But he persuaded the young Latvian to state in his report how, in the course of investigations in Latvia before his arrest, he had bribed certain MVD officers; how he had sent messages through them to his family; how one of these MVD officers had supplied him with news from outside, with cigarettes while he was being interrogated, and so on. All strictly forbidden practices.

This was, of course, untrue, but the ruse was successful —much too successful. The MVD authorities took this confession very seriously, claiming that they could not allow such corruption in their ranks. An investigation was held in distant Latvia, and two of the MVD officers implicated in his arrest were executed.*

But this was not the end. Nearly a year later, our young Latvian friend was accused of having invented the whole story, and he was threatened with execution himself. Harry Anderson now behaved, as he always did, with great courage. He went to the MVD authorities and admitted that he had been responsible for the whole fabrication, which he had persuaded his young countryman to write into his report.

We had warned Harry against starting anything of this

---

*It should be remembered that these MVD men were probably the objects of local jealousy in their own ranks—and that this single denunciation by a prisoner was often quite sufficient to condemn them.

nature, and everything ended badly, as we had feared. The young Latvian was sent to Siberia, his family at home was deported and Harry Anderson paid for his part with his life. I met some Russian soldiers who claimed to have been present at his execution.

15

The Death of Stalin

MARCH 1953

One morning in March 1953, when I had returned for another short spell in the tailors' shop, I was sitting at the bench counting my bits of cloth. A prisoner came over and said quietly as he passed, "The old brute with the moustache is kicking the bucket."

I did not understand and said, "Which old brute?"

"The one with the moustache," he repeated.

This particular prisoner as a rule looked under-nourished and miserable, but this morning his face was positively radiant. I still could not think what he meant, but when I heard him repeating these words to the other prisoners—and saw their faces light up—I realised. He was referring to Stalin! He told us he had heard an official Moscow announcement about the "illness of our great leader" on a wireless belonging to the camp centre.

Within a few minutes everyone was rushing up and down from one section of the workshop to the other, spreading the news. "Illness," in Soviet terms, could mean only one thing—Stalin was already dead, or at any rate dying.

No one produced his norm that morning; even the "recordists'" neglected their work. The whole place seemed upside down, the entire factory in commotion, buzzing like a disturbed beehive. Short of an announce-ment that the British and Americans had landed in

159

Moscow, nothing could have sounded more wonderful. Many people started to sing.

I found it particularly revealing to watch the factory managers and the MVD officials. Some looked pleased, and the faces of one or two revealed a satisfaction similar to ours. Others showed their feelings with embarrassed smiles. Some looked really frightened. It was easy to tell that day who were the faithful servants of the régime.

When we returned to the camp in the evening, all the non-working prisoners were standing at the entrance, waiting to confirm the news. They thought we had not heard it, because there were no loudspeakers in the factories, no music or entertainment of any kind, not even the familiar blasts of propaganda (in the factory we were expected to concentrate to the exclusion of all else on the accursed norm). They told us that all day, with a few interruptions for news bulletins, Radio Moscow had broadcast only funeral marches by Beethoven and Chopin.

This radio programme continued for two days; funeral marches were interspersed every hour with short bulletins about the illness of the dictator which, we now realised, must be fatal. We longed, hoped, prayed that he would die. No one living in the West can have the least idea of how this hope dominated all our thoughts and conversations for the next forty-eight hours. And then, when his death was announced, the beatific smiles, the radiance, the joy on every face!

A day of national mourning was proclaimed, and preparations were made for us all to "mourn with the nation." Red flags draped with black were hoisted on all the official buildings, and we were ordered to behave quietly and soberly. But strange, unheard-of things began to happen. A drunken guard tottered around the camp and muttered to me, "Not only you, but *we* are happy."

An MVD officer we particularly disliked, who was also half-drunk, prattled on about how he hoped the prisoners would understand why he had been so severe; he had had to obey the orders of the inhuman ruler. "His system," he said, "has been as hard on us as on you." And he told us that many guards and MVD officers lived in a state of permanent insecurity, not knowing on what day, at what hour, they too might find themselves not guarding us, but *with* us, fellow-prisoners.

These were pleasing signs. To hear these words from Russian officials filled us with hope; and in the next few weeks discipline was relaxed in an astonishing way. The guards and MVD men became quite friendly, and improvements of various kinds were introduced in our living and working conditions, as well as in our rations. The constant day and night searchings of the barracks stopped. The punitive brigades were disbanded. The solitary confinement *karker* was pulled down. When the order for this last measure was given, the prisoners shouted with joy, and we all helped remove the debris of the building amidst the laughter of the MVD officers and guards.

I must be honest and state here that it was not only Stalin's death which was responsible for these improvements. During the summer of 1952, nine months before, a new government decree had improved our rations and, for the first time, we were paid for our work. This was no more than a kind of pocket money, it is true, but it enabled us to buy a little extra sugar and margarine when they were available.

The brick kilns which had been run by women prisoners, the work being considered too light for men, were now taken over by men. Special camps were opened for the old and crippled and some of the old Russians were sent home.* Many women were released, their camps turned into men's camps, and some of the men's camps were to be, we were assured, "recreation camps." Recreation! The very word sounded thrilling.

That all this was not merely a local improvement in the Dubrov camps, but was general throughout Russia, became clear later when we heard the speeches of Malenkov and Khrushchev, to which we were all invited to listen on the camp loudspeakers. Khrushchev spoke openly of the faults of the system, referring to the "crimes committed by the Stalinist régime!" He admitted that the Soviet Union was unable to compete in quality, or in quantity, with the West. He stated that only shoddy goods were produced in most of the factories, that the yield of the land had fallen year by year. He revealed that the cattle stock had diminished by eight million since 1938, that it was *lower than it had been under the Tsars!* He said it had been madness to enforce centralisation, that only de-centralisation (anathema to the Socialist creed) could, in the present state of Soviet society, produce consumer goods; he admitted that neither food nor clothing arrived on time. In short, he said that the great Communist Party had proved unable to meet the requirements of the Russian people!

I have said that we were already earning a little pocket money. There had seldom been much to spend it on because sugar, margarine and any other fats available in the canteen were sold only to "recordists." But now anyone who fulfilled his norm could buy a pound of sugar and some margarine three times a month. I was also

*It was a terrible comment on Soviet society that often the wives and families of these old people refused to accept them back, on the ground that they could not feed them!

able to buy a little dried fruit and some coarse *mahorka* tobacco.

The brigades were divided into several *razryads*, or work categories, and pay varied according to which *razryad* you were in. Those like myself in the tailors' shop could earn twenty-eight roubles a month, if we produced the norm, which would buy about one and a half pounds of margarine.

Another improvement for the political prisoners was the imposition of the death penalty for murder. Until now, murders in the camp had been punished merely by imprisonment, which had no deterrent effect whatsoever on the bandits. A document announcing this death penalty was handed round, and everyone had to read and sign it. The authorities thereby admitted implicitly that, until now, they had not objected to murder in their camps. Indeed, they had, in my opinion, deliberately encouraged it. Later, capital punishment was also introduced for certain cases of robbery with violence.

But such long-standing habits of violence cannot be eradicated completely. Savagery cannot be wiped out overnight in a land like Russia. The bandits simply became more careful about whom they murdered, and how they murdered them. All the same, the bloody brawls which had often ended in death or permanent disablement diminished.*

Our first, automatic reaction to Stalin's death had been simply, "Thank God! We may now at least survive!" It was no longer certain that we would be left to rot in the camps. Until now, no one had imagined he would ever leave them alive. Our hope had been that the West might finally learn what the Soviet world was, stop making concessions, and that a war might break out. But now we

---

*Brawling, for instance, was now punished by a month's detention in the *karkers*, where these cells still remained.

hoped for a less violent solution—hopes which seemed confirmed when the newspapers* informed us that the cases of all foreign prisoners were to be reinvestigated. Anyone who considered he had been unjustly sentenced, or maltreated in prison, might submit his plea in writing. We were told to seal the envelopes and put them in a special box in the commandant's office, from where they would be sent unopened to Moscow. This caused tremendous excitement, and for days many prisoners would talk of nothing else but of how they were going to draw up their statements. Those who could not write consulted the more literate.

In June 1953 certain categories of younger prisoners were called before the camp commandant and interrogated individually. They were mostly Germans and Hungarians who had been captured in the last stages of the war, after being press-ganged into Hitler's werewolves at the age of fourteen or fifteen, or, in the case of the Hungarians, into the *kopjas* youth detachments. They had been too young for the regular army, and could not, after capture, qualify as prisoners of war, so the Russians had tried them as war criminals. (Strictly, in international law they were partisans, or *maquisards*. The Russians never tired of glorifying the feats of *their* partisans—but partisans on the other side were war criminals.) This opprobrious label was now changed, the youths became

---

**Pravda* and *Isveztia*. These papers generally arrived in the camp five days late. Those who wished could go at certain hours to hear the "news" read out. *Isveztia* was full of lies and naïve propaganda, but by reading between the lines, I learned something about world politics. Some of us also managed to listen to the B.B.C. and the American Radio in Munich. Prisoners who were electricians were often ordered to repair the radio sets of the camp officials. There were always one or two of these under repair and, although it was strictly forbidden, they regularly listened to foreign broadcasts. This had gone on for years.

prisoners of war, and in a month of two were on their way home. In the first weeks of June, three hundred and twenty of these left the camp to be repatriated. We later heard that they had to wait several months in the Lvov collecting centre, where their cases were carefully investigated again, so that many did not reach home until December.

There was something most moving about the departure of these boys. All personal feuds and quarrels were forgotten; the old antipathies between Germans and Poles were temporarily laid aside. And those of us who remained behind came to the gates to see them off and wish them, whatever their nationality, God-speed.

The Germans left first, in groups of four. Turning to wave from time to time, they marched away to the accompaniment of our cheers. When the turn of the Hungarians came, I could barely restrain my tears; these youths had learned by bitter personal experience something of our national destiny and the harsh Hungarian fate. Clutching the little sacks which contained all they possessed, they set off for home; and they too turned to look back and wave at the Hungarians they left behind.

The camp guards, as if understanding our feelings, closed the gates slowly, to give us time to watch them for as long as possible. We stood there trying to follow them with our eyes as they moved away into the distance along the high road. They were like a *fata morgana*, a little group marching away, towards happiness.

16

The Sky Darkens Again: Camp No. 5

JULY 1953

Soon there were rumours that more foreigners would be repatriated and that lists of names were already in the camp commandant's office. All the older ones and women with children under the age of ten had been released, and we hoped that our turn would come soon. But the weeks passed and turned into months, and we were still at our factory benches. We worked half-heartedly, unable even to concentrate on earning our small salaries. The camp authorities, too, seemed uncertain about us; we were "dangerous criminals," sentenced to twenty-five years' hard labour, and they clearly did not know whether to regard us as permanent or not.

On the other hand, the relaxation or "thaw" continued for us all. Small cultural groups were encouraged. Sports and recreations, basket-ball and football, were organised; cinema shows became a regular feature of camp life. Musicians among us were allowed to give concerts. Instead of propaganda films about the *kolkhozes*, Stakhanovites, or the great production achievements of Soviet industry, we saw films about nature and science—the landscape of Central Asia, the Taiga, the fauna and flora of different countries in the Soviet Union, hunting pictures, geological expeditions. There were some excellent films of the Bolshoi and Kirov Ballets, and of the bathing resorts in the Caucasus and on the Black

Sea, where old palaces had been converted into Peoples' convalescent homes. We saw the new hotels in Sochi and Sukhum, the "common people" as tourists on well-organised bus trips and invigorating sea voyages.*

We were also supplied with stage properties, and allowed to construct theatrical décor in the wood workshop. In the cultural groups, anyone could lecture on his own subject, and describe his former activities. Naturally, under the title of "Cultural Lectures," we often had some highly critical economic and political discussions, all of them unfavourable to the Soviet Union.

Another feature of this waiting period concerned the attitude towards sex. I have mentioned how the prisoners who used to meet women, in hospitals and fields, tended to be the younger, more hot-blooded ones. Most of us, the older and middle-aged, were too tired after work to have any sexual urges. But now, with the removal of the constant thought of death, and the improvement in our diet, the natural desires appeared again. Some of the middle-aged prisoners started to call at Camp 10, which now contained the women. Friendships, platonic, sentimental, amorous, were formed; love letters were written, exchanged, somehow conveyed from camp to camp. This was indeed a time of sudden meetings, quick acquaintances, furtive loves . . . I had a German friend called Dietrich who had been kidnapped with his fiancée, and both sentenced as "American spies." His fiancée had worked in the kitchen of Camp 10, where he had rarely been able to see, or even correspond with her, while he had been with us in Camp 14. They were now

*The only objection to this was, as one of the better informed Russian prisoners said, that the happy, carefree tourists we saw in these films were mostly Stakhanovites. The "simple people" holidaying in these beautiful places were mainly Party members.

in daily communication, frequently finding some excuse for meeting.

Then came a curious incident, which I did not understand until some months later, when I was called to Moscow for interrogation in the Lubianka prison. It too was connected, although in a most unusual way, with the improvement of our conditions.

A few months after the first groups of prisoners had been repatriated, a senior MGB intelligence officer from the Dubrov H.Q. came to interview me. I was called to the camp commandant's office in the middle of the night and interrogated through a German-speaking interpreter, a woman from the German colony on the Volga. I was questioned closely, and all my answers were carefully noted.

The questions did not concern me directly, but an old acquaintance called Rosen, who had worked with me at the British Commission in Vienna in 1947. Although a Palestinian by birth, he had become a British subject, and had served in the British Army during the war. He had been kidnapped in Vienna by the Russians in 1950, and was now serving his sentence somewhere in Russia. The MGB official showed me a series of photographs in sets of three, asking me if I recognised any of the people in them. Quite why it was I do not know, but Rosen was always the one in the middle. Although I was suspicious on these occasions, there seemed no point in denying anything, and I admitted I had known him. I wondered if Rosen had said he knew me.

The MGB man kept on comparing my evidence taken in Baden seven years before with statements evidently made by Rosen, as if trying to find contradictions. As my Baden "evidence" had been a complete fabrication by my inquisitors, this was not difficult.

"You maintain that this evidence is not correct then?" he said.

" Certainly," I replied. "It's a tissue of lies. You can start the whole thing again, if you like. We might then arrive at the truth."

"Why haven't you made an application for a review of your case?"

I replied that after what I had been through, I had little confidence in the new clemency of the Soviet Union. I suddenly felt despondent, and while this was being written down, I turned desperately to the female interpreter. "Why are they interrogating me again?" I asked. "What do they want? I wish I were dead."

To which she replied quietly, "You don't want to die now when there's a chance of improving your position. Don't worry! All will be well."

That this jovial, middle-aged Volga German should speak so kindly amazed me; at first I thought she was laying some new trap for me. But I told them the truth about Rosen. I said that he had never had anything to do with espionage. His job had been a subordinate one, like mine, concerned chiefly with the postal services of the British H.Q. in Vienna. I suggested that if they interrogated him again he would confirm this, assuming of course that he was allowed to tell the truth.

The MGB interrogator appeared very surprised. He said that if I were lying, I would damage not only myself but also the interrogators who were now trying to help me. This was an extraordinary remark from a high MGB official, but I said he need not worry; I had told the truth. I added sarcastically that his colleagues had been given the truth seven years before in Baden, but they had ignored it. It had cost me this hell in Russia, not to mention eight months' solitary confinement in Baden being interrogated about a crime I had not committed.

That was almost, but not quite, the end of this curious incident which was, I learned later, concerned with the trial of Beria and his subordinates who had nearly tortured poor Rosen to death.*

At this point, when everything pointed to a continuous improvement in our situation, things took a turn for the worse. The slave traders arrived from the Far East again, evil-looking Mongolian-faced officials. We knew what they were looking for, and we were frightened that there had been another change in policy. Or was it simply Russian illogicality, the muddle-headedness of the Slav?

The slave traders graded all the remaining Russian prisoners, and we could only hope that we, as Europeans, would be omitted from this classification. Then some young Rumanian prisoners were called up, and our first fears seemed justified. For two dreadful days, we lost all hope and saw Siberia before us. But it was a mistake; the Rumanians had been interviewed because they had Slavonic sounding names, and they were sent back to the barracks. The slave traders were selecting only Russians, the young, strong and healthy; anyone over forty or in poor health was rejected. These unfortunate Russians were sent to a large oil refinery near Omsk, and to two new power plants on the rivers Ob and Yenesei in Siberia.

Unfortunately, the Balts were considered as Russians and a number of our friends were in this group. A heart-breaking and pathetic leave-taking followed. It was a personal tragedy for me, as it meant a break with the Lithuanian poet, Mishkinis, who had become one of my closest friends and had many of the same endearing qualities as his fellow-countryman Antonos Bruzhas.

*To-day Rosen is in Vienna.

These were days of sadness for all of us. After so many years together, we had forgotten how attached we had become, how much we were a part of one another's lives, how much we trusted one another.

About five hundred of these young men left the camp knowing that they had a long journey before them, because they were accompanied by an armed escort.* Special railway wagons had arrived, well provisioned with food and fuel for a three weeks' journey. This was understandable. These men were a valuable commodity, prize bulls to be kept in fighting trim.

A few weeks later, while we were still waiting anxiously, we heard that our camp was to be turned over to women and that we were to be transferred. Only the essential technicians were to remain, thirty-five men, mostly cutters and designers in the tailors' shop. The rest of us were regrouped, loaded into railway wagons, and sent to the new and, we hoped, temporary camp before repatriation.

As we left, we saw the women arriving, and those who had envied the men who stayed behind changed their minds. Most of the women were old and crippled peasants with handkerchiefs tied around their heads. They were a pathetic sight. What, I wondered, could have been the "crime" of these wretched creatures? They probably knew nothing of politics; they did not even know why they were here. We waved, and some of them waved back wearily. It was my last view of Camp 14.

A number of friends and acquaintances were delighted

---

*Whenever a group of prisoners left for another camp, the authorities of the new camp would send an escort. The escorting guards this time were Easterners, from the most distant parts of Russia.

to see us in the new camp, No. 5. Those who had been there some time and worked indoors tried to persuade their brigadiers that we were particularly suited to work with them, efficient, skilled, reliable, and so on. Had circumstances been different, one might almost have described these happy greetings, these back-slappings and embracings, as an old school reunion.

But unfortunately, these generous attempts to put us on indoor work were unsuccessful, because the camp commandant disliked foreigners. He intended that the newcomers should have the worst jobs. We were not allowed in the shop, which produced radio cabinets, furniture, chess-sets and similar woodwork—and for which some of us were, by now, particularly apt. Although winter had arrived, we were allotted to the brickyards.

Nowhere else in the world do brickyards operate in the winter, because the bricks do not set properly, and it is uneconomical. But such was the need for building material in Russia that these brickyards operated all the year round, sometimes in temperatures of thirty or forty degrees below zero.

Our Hungarian predecessors had been unwittingly responsible for this, not because they had worked badly, but because they had worked well—too well, as the commandant mentioned in his opening speech: "I hope you will be worthy successors of your departed compatriots." Other prisoners told us that the work of one Hungarian in the brickyard equalled that of four other prisoners. Our fellow countrymen had become norm maniacs.

We had to hew the clay with pick-axes from open cast mines as hard as rock. We then pushed it in trucks to an elevator belt which took it up to the factories. Many tons had to be carted daily, and there were several accidents.

It was unfortunate, too, that the medical services of Camp 5 were in the hands of equally vindictive officials. Some of our friends said that these officials were envious because they suspected that we would one day go home. The head of the medical staff was a woman major,* a stunted cripple, who was said to be jealous of anyone with a normal body. If we fell ill or had an accident at work, we could not expect much from her. Her principle appeared to be that no one with a temperature of under 100 should be admitted to hospital. We had a number of tubercular prisoners in our group, who lived in a perpetual state of low fever, with a temperature which never quite reached 100 degrees. Their long, half feverish illness continued while they worked in the brickyards, and when the acute stage of the disease set in, it was too late. Some died in hospital a few weeks after admission.

The only encouraging feature of these months in Camp 5 was that we were told "the judicial committee of the Supreme Soviet has granted correspondence rights to foreigners." In simple language, this meant that we could write one postcard a month to friends and relations at home. Our families had not had word from us since 1947, and the effect on our morale was tremendous. We were given a Moscow camp number, a personal sub-number, and the cards had a blank reply sheet for our correspondents; we were also warned that if we wrote anything objectionable the card would be destroyed, and we would not be notified. I remember how difficult it was, after so many years without writing, to fill up these cards. It took me three days to compose mine, and as I wrote my hand shook.

We now received what seemed another set-back. A

---

*Women wore military uniform, epaulettes and badges of rank like the ordinary MVD.

group of Germans, the young military prisoners of war who had been released some months before, now arrived back in our camp, together with many youths who had been captured during the East Berlin uprising of 17th July, 1953. They had been on their way home, had almost left Russia, when the authorities had changed their minds; they were now being sent to work in Siberia. They were in despair, convinced that, after the Berlin affair, there had been a sudden deterioration in the international situation and that the period of relaxation was over. We had noticed, too, that new lists of foreigners to be repatriated were not being posted. After nine months of hope and longing, since that great day when Stalin died, were we soon to find ourselves back where we were before?

Then when things looked black indeed, my personal salvation arrived.

17

Summoned to Moscow

JANUARY 1954

On the evening of the 10th January, 1954, one of the assistants in the *nariarchiks'* office, a Latvian boy to whom I used to teach English secretly, ran into our hut excitedly. When he saw me, he came up smiling and said I was to go to the central store and change into new clothes—*without a number!* He stood there blinking, I remember now how happy the boy, a prisoner himself, was on my behalf. "Isn't it wonderful!" he said. "You're being freed. We've had special instructions to prepare you for a journey. You leave at five o'clock to-morrow."

I could hardly believe my ears as friends came up to congratulate me. I did not sleep much that night, because they were constantly coming over to my bunk with the names and addresses of relations they wanted me to visit, or communicate with, in the West. Everyone, even the Germans, asked me to take messages. It would have been unwise to write down names, so I tried to memorise them. But such was my excitement that, although my memory had greatly improved during imprisonment, I had soon forgotten every one of them.

The next morning my friends came to the camp gates to see me off, and one of them, an old Ukrainian priest, insisted on giving me his rosary. As I walked away, I looked back on their faces at the gates, happy and smiling, waving until I was out of sight; and I felt a lump rise in my throat. They were happy for my sake—but what about their future? The two guards who accompanied me were armed with tommy-guns, but they too were in the best of spirits. One of them kept laughing and repeating, "*Domoy! Domoy!*" (Home! Home!) I was deeply touched that all these people who lived in the camps were prepared to forget their own troubles because of my good fortune.

I was taken first to Camp 18 at Potyma, a large railway junction on the Moscow-Kuibyshev main line. This was a good sign, as it was a receiving and distributing centre for prisoners in the entire Dubrov area, with a section for prisoners about to be repatriated. But on arrival I was placed in the quarantine section among prisoners who had just arrived, about to start their sentences. By some error the new arrivals were put with those about to be freed, thereby increasing the sadness of the former, and diminishing the joy of the latter.

The following morning I was called before the camp commandant who told me that I was to be interviewed by "very important people." He recommended me to keep my mouth shut about conditions in the Dubrov camps. "You may have to return here," he said. "And if you don't behave yourself, we shall know how to take care of you when you come back."

I was appalled by this, and realised from his reference to "very important people," that I was still far from being freed.

I spent three weeks in this camp, and was then taken one morning with a small group of prisoners to the Potyma railway station, to be put on a west-bound train. But when the train arrived it had no prisoners' compartments, and we were marched back to the camp, to wait for the same train the next day. And this train too was so full of prisoners that there was no room for us, so we again had to return to the camp. This procedure was repeated on four consecutive days, until finally the authorities, who evidently wanted at all costs to get rid of us, put us on the first train with prisoner compartments which came in, regardless of its destination. They evidently calculated that we might find a station somewhere on the way, where there *might* be some empty carriages, and they *might* be going in the right direction. Such are Russian methods. In this way we travelled *east* for three days, towards the Volga, finally arriving at Kuibyshev! Here we spent several days in the local prison, and were then marched to the station and locked into some wagons. Twenty-four hours later the train began to move. Judging from the position of the sun, we were at last going west.

In spite of this muddle, the method of locking us in the wagons was efficient enough. The prisoners' carriages were divided into several compartments, each with a grille door giving on to the corridor, and there were no windows. The outside of the coach was made of sheet metal, but the interior was of wood, containing benches and four-tier bunks. The grilles were fastened with multiple locks, as in ordinary gaols. These prison wagons were an important and essential part of Russian rolling-stock, and were used in conjunction with the ordinary goods service. But when the journey was urgent, as in our case, these wagons would be attached to a transcontinental passenger train. In this way, we travelled along next to coaches full of civilian passengers—by Pullman as it were. Does such a train exist anywhere else in Europe?

We continued like this for three days, the train stopping at rural stations to pick up new groups of prisoners. They were mostly peasants, clerks, accountants from the collective farms, who had been arrested for speculation or falsification of accounts. There were also a number of real hardened criminals among them, in chains. The various kinds of prisoner were carefully segregated in the wagons. The common criminals, or *bitovoys* as they were called, were separated from us, the political prisoners; and the men and women were in different compartments.

Only four of us came from the Dubrov camps, two elderly Russians, a young Russian soldier and myself. The old Russians were being taken to a nursing home in Moscow, because their peasant families had refused to have them back at home. In the neighbouring compartment were a number of women prisoners, mostly *bitovoys* convicted of common crimes, pickpockets and prostitutes. They spent the time singing coarse songs and provoking the guards. Our compartment was next to the lavatory, and we could see everyone who passed. One of these female *bitovoys* on her way there provocatively flaunted her breasts under a camp greatcoat. This caused a great flurry among the younger male prisoners.

One evening when she was on her way to the lavatory, she moved close to the door, and allowed the young Russian soldier in our compartment to fondle her through the grille. The amorous sounds they made, continued for at least five minutes, waking up the guard who was dozing at the end of the corridor. He started shouting but the *bitovoy* flung back some obscenities, suggesting that, if he were envious, he might take his turn.

Knowing the guards, I was not surprised that he took advantage of this. Towards dawn the following morning I woke, to see them openly making love in the corridor. I slept near the grille door, and one of the other young Russians who was also awake, pleaded with me to change bunks, so that he could have a better view. He became immensely excited, hysterical with lust. Finally, the girl took pity on him. After she had left the guard, she came close to the grille and allowed him to repeat the performance through the bars.

After four days, the Russians in our compartment announced that we were approaching Moscow. They had been allowed to look out through the bars of the corridor window, and on my excursions to the lavatory I managed to take a glance. It was a barren landscape. A few old wooden huts, cottages and dilapidated collective farms were the only signs of human habitation; not a house, not a man, not even an animal was in sight. We might have been on the moon. When we approached Moscow a few people and houses appeared, but both looked equally forlorn.

We were nearly an hour in the suburbs, and the train seemed to make a complete detour of the city, finally stopping at a grimy station where we alighted on an empty platform. Here we were immediately surrounded by a posse of Security police, who separated us into groups, and allotted us to waiting black armoured vans. We were put in the front, but through the window of the rear part, which was occupied by the guards, I had my first glimpse of Moscow. Here at last was the Communist Holy City, the Mecca of those millions all over the world, idealists some of them, naïve idiots most of them, who believe in Communism.

The people in the streets stared at our van, which had priority over all other vehicles. They had no doubt seen a Black Maria before. As we approached the centre of the city, I noticed that the people looked very different from the Russians I had known during my seven years in the country, the "free" Russians outside the camps. They were better dressed, in fur hats, heavy overcoats and solid boots. The coarse quilted overalls which were such a feature in the country and the camps had disappeared.

The van stopped several times to deposit prisoners at various gaols; they were in different parts of the city, and the receiving process at each was very slow. The roundabout journey took two hours. At last, we crossed a bridge and the outlines of the Kremlin appeared. We passed a number of low buildings and I remember seeing two old ladies in the road behind, one of whom noticed our van and drew her friend's attention to it. The two women stared and then quickly turned away, walking off without looking back. The arrival of a black van at the tall building ahead evidently meant much to them. I did not know that we were arriving at the infamous Lubianka prison.

18

The Lubianka Prison

FEBRUARY 1954

The notoriety of this prison dates from the earliest days of the Bolshevist revolution when it was the headquarters of the Cheka* and later of the OGPU. Its chief in those days (1922) was Dzerzhinsky, who was responsible for the execution of many thousands of "class enemies" within its walls.

A Russian Socialist once said that fate itself had provided in advance for the interests of the Cheka by establishing a building in the very heart of Moscow which was hermetically sealed by lofty walls. It was built by an insurance company in Tsarist times. When it was taken over by the Cheka, they installed cells and fitted out cellars underneath the internal courtyards. Prisoners were executed in the cellars while lorry engines were revved up to drown the noise of the shots. It was only during the last war that large additions were made to turn the Lubianka into a kind of fortress.

From the outside it looks like any of the big buildings in the centre of Moscow. Nearby are the Science and Education Ministry, the theatre and several foreign Embassies. The result is that it presents a harmless, even a friendly appearance from outside. But this impression changes immediately its threshold is crossed.

The identity cards and documents of our driver and

*The original Communist secret police.

guards, as well as the prisoners', were examined at the gate, and again when we entered the main courtyard. Before an interior building, whose entrance at the head of an impressive marble staircase consisted of copper-sheeted double doors, I was told to get out. My documents were handed over to an MVD officer, who immediately asked me, "Have you been well treated?" and, "Has anything been stolen from you?" I said I had no complaints, and he escorted me into a small windowless room. He asked if I was hungry, and I told him that I was, as I had eaten only salted herring and black bread on the journey. He smiled and said I should have a meal immediately.

This officer, a captain, reassured me with his friendly manner, for I was by now a little apprehensive. He went out, and a man in a smart chef's uniform brought me an aluminium bowl containing fish soup and something resembling macaroni. Having never eaten anything like this for eight years, I had almost forgotten that such food existed. As I ate, my stomach seemed to glow and expand.

I was left alone in this room for over an hour, and I sat there determined to be optimistic. All this must surely lead to my release. But memories of the past eight years kept on returning. All the sad and tragic events of my captivity passed before my mind, and I remembered those fleeting moments of happiness with my friends, Antonos Bruzhas, Harry Anderson, Miklos Csomos — they all came flooding back, and they seemed to me already memories of some distant dream world. Had I really lived through it all?

For the last nine months I had looked only forward, shutting the door on the past, refusing to remember it, the barbed wire, the working brigades, the palisades, the *karker*, the grey monotony of prison life. I thought, too, of the departure of those Hungarian boys returning home, the unforgettable look on their faces as they left; then, less reassuring, of those other Hungarians I had left behind, smiling, waving as I too left. They had believed I was returning home. But here I was, in the Lubianka prison in Moscow. What was going to happen to me?

I was daydreaming like this, when an orderly came in and told me to follow him. I accompanied him, in a daze, hardly daring to hope that this would continue, half afraid that something unforeseen would plunge me back into my tortured dream-world.

An officer and two n.c.o.s met us outside and took me across the courtyard to a tall seven-story building in the middle of the square. This, too, was closely guarded, and all of us, my escorts included, were allowed to enter only after our documents had been examined again. The security arrangements inside, along a labyrinth of corridors, were equally elaborate. A number of multi-coloured lights were continually flashing, and whenever a certain colour appeared, it indicated, I learnt later, either that an important MVD officer was passing, or that another prisoner was being taken through the corridors. When this happened, I was made to turn and keep my face to the wall. This prison was unlike any other I had seen in Russia, clean, well-swept, eerily silent due to the rubber floors, and staffed by guards in well-cut green uniforms which reminded me of the old German Imperial *Waffenrock*.

We went up several flights of stairs, and I was handed over to a gaoler who smiled in an equally friendly way, warning me at the same time that I must talk quietly. He spoke in whispers, and I suddenly felt, in this sepulchral atmosphere, that I had entered some kind of new twentieth-century Gothic cathedral.

My cell, which was larger than any I had had before, contained a camp bed and table. High on the wall was a large grille window, most of which was covered by a plank, so that only a patch of sky was visible at the top. The cell was centrally heated by a radiator behind an iron screen.

The gaoler asked if I smoked, and I told him that my pipe was in my bag which had been taken at the gates. He said that I would be allowed all my personal possessions, and would be provided with a daily tobacco ration. The only time I could be in bed was between retreat at night and reveille in the morning, and if I wanted anything, I was to raise my arm when the guard passed my window. If I had any complaints I was to make them.

In spite of this civilised reception, I was still apprehensive. I had hoped that the visit to Moscow would be connected with my release. Perhaps I had been too optimistic. I cursed myself for having asked one of the first young Hungarians to be repatriated some months before to take a message to some friends in England. Perhaps he had not been released. Perhaps they had cross-examined him and he had told them of my message?

After three days, the gaoler asked me if I would like to read. As Hungarian books were not available, I asked for English and German authors. He brought me a curious selection, including a medieval religious romance by E. Wiechert about Heinrich von Plauen, the last Grand Master of the German Catholic Knights. Another dealt with modern aspects of democracy, but from a Communist point of view. I also re-read *Oliver Twist* in English, a bowdlerised version, concentrating largely on the poverty in nineteenth-century England.

I was allowed daily exercise. A special exercise track had been constructed on the seventh floor of my prison block, at the end of which stood two guards armed with tommy-guns. As I walked here I was aware of the streets of Moscow below; they were not visible, but the noise and hubbub of a great city surged up. This kind of remote proximity to the capital of the people who had oppressed me for eight years was so dispiriting that I decided to abandon these exercises in favour of my solitary cell, with only my books and thoughts for company. But fears of all kinds, self-created fears no doubt, continually possessed me. When a prisoner is left alone in a cell, even if the treatment is good, his imagination becomes extraordinarily fertile. At one point I remember I became distracted because the reply postcard which I had sent to my family from Camp 5 had not been returned. I wondered if they had received it, or if I had written something which had involved me in fresh trouble.

I lost count of the days, but weeks must have passed, during which I did not speak a word. Time seemed to have stopped. Only the regular lowering of the hatch when the guard looked in through the grille, or deposited my food, gave event to my life. Worried and tired, unable to concentrate, I even began to lose interest in reading.

One day I was taken to the prison dentist and I imagined that my teeth, which were in very poor condition, would be repaired. His surgery was well-equipped with modern American appliances. But all he wanted was to make an inventory of my teeth and record the topography of my mouth.

Hallucinations now began to afflict me, accompanied by strange buzzings and hummings in my head. I heard, or thought I heard, high-pitched, then low-pitched, sounds. At night, a curious tinkling music came to me. I wondered if these sounds were perhaps inner voices, the result of some neurosis or derangement of mind, the effect perhaps of my cerebral hæmorrhage? Was I going mad? After seven years of prison life had I lost my reason?*

At last, after many weary weeks, the door of my cell opened one morning and a new gaoler came in and whispered, "*Kak familiya?*"—"What's your name?" I said: "Rupert." "*Podyom!*"—"Come on!" He led me downstairs to the door and handed me over to two guards who were waiting for me. They took me across the central courtyard, and into a large building with elaborate wrought-iron gates. Here, I found myself in a veritable palace. The wood-panelled corridors were full of Samarkand and Tashkent carpets. Expensive French paintings, furniture and console tables lined the walls. I did not know it at the time, of course, but this was the Holy of Holies, the headquarters of the MGB Secret Police.

I was escorted into an office which was equally well furnished, with leather arm-chairs and plush carpets, where I was confronted at a desk by a fat Russian Air Force officer who looked like Goering. He wore the official Communist smile and was extremely jovial. He dismissed the guard and offered me a cigarette. "*Kak dyela!*"—"How are you?" he said, motioning me to one of the easy-chairs. He spoke Russian, and asked why I had not learnt the language during my stay in his country. I could speak a little, but I told him frankly that apart from not having much inclination, learning foreign languages in the camps had been forbidden.

---

*I was later told that these sounds could have been produced by the so-called *yagoda* siren, a horn emitting high-pitched notes calculated to grate on the prisoner's nerves, invented by Yagoda, one of the first chiefs of the Soviet security police in the early days of Communism.

He smiled. "What a pity you didn't learn our language!"

"I was not allowed to," I repeated.

"That was a mistake," he said.

He sent for an interpreter, and said he wanted me to tell him everything about myself, my prison experiences, my state of health, my treatment, my likes and dislikes—in short, whatever I felt about life. He was kindness personified; but his joviality did not reassure me. What did he want? If I was to be pardoned and released, why had I been brought before this man, in this noiseless prison?

The interpreter, a tall immaculately-dressed officer, came in and asked what languages I spoke. I said that my previous interrogations by the Russians in Baden had been in German, but that they had been faultily transcribed.

" Rest assured," he replied in excellent German, "all you say will be translated faithfully. It will be read out to you before it is put on record."

I was far from convinced. "Good God!" I thought. "After seven years of prison, here are records, minutes and interrogations again!"

We now moved to a round table and sat in leather arm-chairs, smoking cigarettes. The Russian Air Force officer again made inquiries about the conditions in the camps I had been in. He asked if there were great differences in the treatment of prisoners in the various camps, how they compared with this prison, and so on. His civility and jokes about my time in Russia seemed to make a mockery of all I had gone through. It also made me suspicious.

He asked me if I needed anything. I said I had no money.

"Well, you shall have some," he said. "What make of tobacco do you like?"

"*Mahorka*," I replied automatically.

They both laughed, and suggested that I might like something better.

"No," I said. "I'm used to *mahorka* now. I've been smoking it for years."

Knowing that Russian promises mean next to nothing, I was very sceptical, particularly when they retreated into a corner and talked in whispers. When the interpreter came back, he asked me if I knew why I was here. I said I did not.

" I will explain then," he said. " You are going to be cross-examined as a witness. We need your testimony. You must be very careful to tell the truth, and nothing but the truth. I must warn you that if you commit perjury, you are liable to a further two years' imprisonment. We don't want you to be frightened of talking about anyone, however important he may be. Or whatever his nationality. Russians included. A general, a colonel, anyone. All we want is the truth."

I could not think what this meant. I had heard that several high-ranking officers had been arrested, Hungarians, Germans and French; but they had already been tried, and were in prison.

"Who is this important officer?" I asked.

"It is not for you to ask questions," he said, smiling, "that is our business."

I suddenly recognised on the interrogator's desk the original records of my interrogations in Baden years before, neatly bound in a volume. It was then that I began to suspect what it was all about. Some of the pages were marked, and the fat air force officer began turning them over. He read out various passages, asking how true they were. I told him that they were a pack of lies.

I had admitted, apparently, having organised a spy ring and several secret agents, and had been in Italy for this purpose—a country I had never visited in my life! Having admitted all this, he said, did I not consider that I had deserved my sentence?

"I made no such admissions," I said.

He continued to ask me what my spy activities had been. "You have confessed it yourself," he said. "Here," he tapped the document, and read out further monstrous statements I was supposed to have made in Baden. "You state that this is all untrue then? With a clear conscience?"

"Of course," I said. "With the clearest conscience."

"But how is it possible?" he said, affecting to be surprised. "This is your own personal record. Try to think hard. Try to remember. Perhaps after all these years, your memory is not reliable. You may have forgotten what you said."

"I know perfectly well what I said."

He read out further passages in which I had apparently mentioned the names of relations and friends in Vienna, together with members of the British Mission. These had been social and domestic contacts, but my Baden interrogators had obviously interpreted them in their own way, trying to incriminate these people because they had known me.

They watched me carefully, as each name was read out. These men were experts in interrogation, and they realised that my surprise was not feigned. "We don't want you to be frightened," the air force officer said at last. "You must realise that you cannot be sentenced for the same crime again. Nothing can make your situation worse. But a lot can make it better." They went across to the corner and they put their heads together again.

When they returned they laid aside the Baden records

and picked up another volume. This was my statement taken the year before, in Camp 14, in July, about Sergeant Rosen. They asked me about him, and I repeated what I had said—that he had been no more than a simple postal clerk, whom I had known at the British H.Q. in Vienna.

"You can find out everything very easily," I said. "Because Rosen was shanghaied by your Russians. You can compare our statements."

It was now becoming clearer how I was to be used as a witness. As I realised later, I was playing a part in one of the biggest criminal cases of all times, against Beria and his secret police. Accusations against his organisation, on account of its brutal methods, had started in 1953, and investigations were still going on. Neither the case of Sergeant Rosen, nor mine, nor that of any other of the unimportant prisoners whom these men were now interrogating so carefully, would otherwise have been worth all this trouble.

Some two hundred foreign witnesses like myself had been brought to Moscow, solely to help in the preparation of the charges. Proof was required about the cruelty of Beria's men, the interrogations and tortures of the Stalinist period. What better witnesses than the victims themselves? And the false documents claiming to explain their cases, the fictitious minutes? These minutes were now causing considerable embarrassment to their authors, because the new régime under Khrushchev wanted to find out the truth about the tens of thousands of foreign prisoners on their hands, nearly all accused of espionage. Only some of these, a very small proportion, were spies, and they wanted to get rid of the others by repatriating them. The problem was to find out who was who.

These inquiries into Rosen's case continued for days. They also asked me about my relations with a man called Billy Bauer, an Austrian business-man, who had been my guest several times at the British officers' club. They appeared quickly satisfied with my replies about him, and soon returned to Rosen. My interrogator observed that I was now saying exactly what I had said eight months before, in Camp 14—and not what had been recorded in the Baden minutes. They were impressed by this. Had I not been telling the truth, I could not have repeated almost word for word my statement in Camp 14. "You learnt your lesson well eight months ago," the air force officer said, smiling.

" There was no need to learn it," I said.

" Then you deny the validity of the whole of your original statement? Either we accept your second statement, or we accept the original one. We have to come to a decision on one of them. That is why we intend going into details." They then again asked if there was anything I wanted? I said I was tired of solitary confinement; I would like a cell companion.

The next day I was put in a cell with a young Russian officer. I was naturally suspicious that he might be the familiar stool pigeon, but after two days' conversation, in German, I thought he was sincere and I liked him.

He told me he had always been a faithful Communist, a Komsomol member in his youth, educated at the Moscow Military Academy; later he had become a major on the general staff, and had been wounded in the war. Then he was arrested—he did not know what for—and taken away from his wife, after three days of married life. He had already been in prison four and a half years.

I felt extremely sorry for him; he was very bitter, and said that you could never trust your friends in Russia, because it was the intrigues of "friends" which had landed him in gaol, on trumped-up charges. But things were better now and, as in my case, the illegality of his sentence was being investigated. We tried to cheer one another up by saying that both of us would soon be free.

One evening, we listened to jet planes flying over Moscow in preparation for the May Day celebrations. It was the first time that I had heard the sound of a jet and he explained that these were the new "reactive" aeroplanes. I found this piece of news disconcerting. If Soviet industry could make these ghastly things too, then the war for which we all hoped, might not necessarily end in a Western victory.* Every evening between seven and eight p.m. we listened to the bangs and shrieks of these jet planes.

While we were together, an important Government commission, consisting of several officers led by a general, came round and talked to us, as usual in a most amiable manner. The general showed great interest in me, and I had the feeling that my name was not unfamiliar to him. He told me that he was Deputy Chief Public Prosecutor, and that I might tell him anything I wished. I told him I was here as witness, and that I was guilty of nothing.

"Well, if you consider you are not guilty," he said, "you have presumably appealed for a revision of your case?"

I said I had not because I had little confidence in the new régime. This did not appear to annoy him, and he smiled. "Would you like your case to be re-examined—fairly, I mean?" he asked.

I thanked him and said that, as I had been here for weeks and they were evidently going through all my

---

*From what we had picked up in the Russian newspapers in the camps, we were delighted that the Americans were surrounding the Soviet Union with hundreds of military bases, and we hoped this would lead to war. The Soviet newspapers identified at least four hundred and twenty of these bases.

evidence again, though clearly in connection with another case, they might as well look into mine if they liked. He said that my case was quite well known by now.

Not long after this, my Russian cell companion left and I found myself alone again. It is extraordinary how stimulating it is to have a companion after weeks of solitary confinement. It took me several days to return to my old melancholy. Perhaps meanwhile, I told myself, they were really re-investigating my case?

At the next interrogation, I asked the air force officer if they would get it all over, and if I were not to be released, to be sent back to the Dubrov camps. I explained that I had been in the camps so long now that I liked the company of prisoners. I had begun to feel that prisoners were the only human beings with whom I now had a common language; I would probably feel ill at ease with free men.

They laughed, assuring me that it would not take so long as in the past, and they asked me to be patient. I would perhaps have to spend two or three weeks more here, but they would do what they could for me.

I had several more interrogations, always on the same theme, the divergence between my various statements about Sergeant Rosen and his activities in Vienna. The interrogators still tried to confuse and embarrass me by constantly confronting the two statements, and they occasionally mentioned the possibility of two years' imprisonment for perjury—but in a half-hearted way, laughing as they said it. (I learned later that the chief interrogator was very satisfied with my answers, which were used extensively in the charges against Beria's assistants.)

Finally they asked about the methods employed in my previous interrogations in Baden. What kinds of torture or physical punishment had been used? How much time had I spent in solitary confinement? Under what conditions? How had the proceedings of the military tribunal been conducted? With or without a defending counsel? They also wanted to know the exact punishments I had undergone since my arrest. The *karker*. Who were the perpetrators of such atrocities? Did I know their names? I was delighted to tell them all about the AVO headquarters, Andrassy Ut 60 in Budapest, where I had been beaten up. At this they looked at one another and shook their heads, in horror or was it mock horror?

"Only the Hungarians were cruel?" asked the interrogator. "What about the Russians in Baden? Who left you for ten months alone in a wet, cold cellar with no exercise? What about *their* interrogations ? And their prison cells, where there was hardly room to stand?"

"Hypocrites," I thought. For I still felt convinced that these men had behaved exactly the same themselves under Stalin's régime. Perhaps they had not tortured people, but they had certainly believed in the "let them rot alive in wet and putrid cells" methods of interrogation.

"Now we know how our people behaved in occupied territories," they said piously to one another. "In Vienna, Budapest, Bucharest!" The fat interrogator put up his hands in horror. "Don't I know it! Don't I know it!"

It was an interesting spectacle.

I suddenly felt quite weak and faint. Perhaps these men were not hypocrites. Was it possible, I wondered as I looked at them closely, that Stalin's death could really have brought about such a change? Perhaps the West and Russia could now meet on common ground. Perhaps a general reconciliation was already in progress. I realised that I was being treated with understanding, almost as an ally. Perhaps I had really achieved something, in helping condemn the methods of the Stalin régime in the occupied territories.

They knew of the conversation about the reopening of my case with the deputy public prosecutor in my cell, and asked me where I would go if I were released. They did not appear shocked when I said Great Britain. They seemed well disposed and said we must all hope for the best; but they refused to commit themselves about my future.

The minutes of the questions and answers were then brought, in translation, for me to sign. I read them carefully, found that they were accurate, and willingly signed, at the top and bottom of each page. So ended after more than three months a further series of wearying interrogations, which I had at first imagined would be concerned only with my liberty and return to Hungary.

It was the 28th April, 1954, over a year after the death of Stalin, when I left Lubianka, still not knowing my destination.

III. WESTWARD

1954-1956

19

The Long Road Home

MAY 1954

I was in a prisoners' train going east, bound, I soon realised, for the world of the camps. As I looked out through the scratches on the frosted glass in the corridors, I saw that we were returning to a land I knew. I recognised the junction at Potyma; then we turned off south towards the Dubrov area.

Although completely disillusioned by this visit to Moscow, I looked forward to seeing old friends again and telling them about my abortive visit to the great Lubianka, of the interrogators who adopted the new "civilised" approach, while ingeniously using me for their own advantage. "I am a pawn," I said to myself, "and no one cares what happens to pawns. Pawns can quite easily die at work, one cold day in the winter."

I saw ahead again the working brigades, less brutal perhaps, but still working brigades. I saw the endless *proverkas* in the early mornings, the standing about in the Russian snow waiting for something that is nothing. Was this really to be my destiny? I, a western man, who had known civilisation, who was still anxious to achieve something in life—was this the point of it all? Was this why I had been born on this planet?

I was not taken back to my old camp. There was an order, of which I was unaware, that no prisoner should return to one in which he had been before. Instead, I was

199

taken to a small camp containing about five hundred prisoners, mostly technicians repairing railway engines and wagons, while the less qualified, like myself, were employed on staining railway sleepers with creosote.

It was unhealthy work. Creosote contains a powerful alkali, whose smell in the heat becomes overpowering, and it sometimes made me feel quite sick. We worked with an automatic stainer, which affected the skin. Hands and faces became swollen as a result of contact with the creosote, and if water gets on to the skin the itch is unbearable. My body was soon a mass of blisters, and my skin black. How unhealthy this work was can be imagined from the fact that we were given half a litre of milk a day, some to be drunk before, some after work. I had never drunk milk before in Russia and did not know that it existed. A prisoner friend, a doctor, told me that milk absorbs the alkali and other tar products which have entered the body, thus protecting the breathing organs, the glands and mucous membranes.

Hard as this work was, I must state, in fairness, that conditions for the prisoners continued to improve. Our working day was never more than ten hours, and the food was much better. We were allowed to write and receive a postcard a month. Red Cross parcels, one of the greatest boons imaginable for a prisoner, began arriving. I shall not forget the generosity of countries like Austria and Western Germany who came to the relief, not only of their own people, but of us all. Every day a hundred and fifty of these parcels arrived,* each weighing from ten to sixteen pounds, containing food, clothes and medicine.

The food in the parcels was of the highest quality, and very soon all the prisoners were looking better. We

---

*Called *posilka* in Russian, one of the few words of that language I never wish to forget.

even managed to send the names of Russian prisoners who were our friends to the Red Cross, and they too received the parcels. If we shared our parcels with everyone, it meant, on an average about one parcel to every ten prisoners, or the equivalent of a pound and a half of extra food per person per day. The parcels also contained a receipt coupon which the addressee filled in as an acknowledgment, and returned to the camp centre. The number of parcels arriving daily finally became so great that auxiliary personnel had to be recruited at the camp post office to deal with them. A further concession was that those who wished to cook the contents of their parcels were allowed to build themselves a small kitchen. Whether as a result of the new policy, or of the general improvement in Russia, I do not know, but the postal and camp authorities were scrupulously honest with these parcels. There were few complaints about theft or loss.

Another feature of the relaxations was the sport and recreation now encouraged. One day I accompanied our camp football team when they went to play another camp, and to my intense pleasure found Antonos Bruzhas among the spectators. I told him about my Lubianka experiences and he said, "Of course anything can happen in Russia. But I believe this will lead to your release. And not to Siberia. Where incidentally I want to go now."

"You want to go to *Siberia*!"

Whereupon he took some photographs from his pocket and showed me his wife and sons and two grandchildren playing with a bear cub. They had been deported to Siberia, but were reasonably contented. He had just heard from them, and had applied to join them there. "Perhaps I can play the organ there, in a Siberian village!"

I relate this incident because it is the only case I know

of anyone actually wanting to go to Siberia. Much later, I heard that his wish was granted; he is presumably there to-day.

I also found myself with Miklos Csomos again and the Hungarian politician, Bela Kovacs. Miklos had been sacked from his hospital job on account of "dishonesty." He had been asked to fill the teeth of certain Russian officials (Secret Police and camp staff) with brass—for gold was unobtainable. Unfortunately however, they actually supplied him with copper which had oxidised in their mouths, and several of them had been badly poisoned. For this quite unintentional mistake he had done a long spell in the *karker*, and here he was now, in an ordinary working brigade, irrepressible as ever. "So many Russians the less!" he laughed about the copper teeth.

But all these improvements and concessions did not compensate for my unsuccessful visit to Moscow. It was now nearly a year since the first prisoners had been sent home, and here I was, still in a Russian concentration camp.

An interesting feature of Russian psychology was revealed in the new Khrushchev era. Our camp contained many Russian prisoners, from all social layers—if one may use that term in a supposedly egalitarian society—from the highest intellectuals and army officers down to the poorest *moujiks*. All these Russians naturally detested the régime which had imprisoned them; but when Khrushchev, the prototype of the *moujik*, came to power and told them about their grievances in a language comprehensible to everyone, speaking strongly against the past iniquities, the nepotism and injustice of the Stalinist régime, they became mesmerised by his words. Even intelligent professors, who until now had been the bitterest opponents of the régime, often surpassing us in their hatred of it, could talk of nothing else.

In this new atmosphere it seemed as if their violent feelings had swung in an extraordinary volte-face to the other extreme, into a kind of burning Slavonic passion. Before, they had talked only of Western help and the "liberation" they longed for. Now they began to boast of how the Russian nation had at last come into its own. "We have found our soul!" they cried. "Now the West will see what a creative, energetic nation can and will achieve!"

One fanatic said to me: "You Westerners will soon realise the magnificent results which will now derive from the Russian craving for work. You will have to recognise our supremacy. The great eternal Russia is at last resurrected. The vocation for which destiny intended us will at last be accomplished. You, nations and sons of the West, will one day see what our reborn country can do. And Russia will work in the interests of all humanity! In *your* interests too!"

Here we have the true Russian, a creature governed only by his emotions. In the strange ferment of ideas unloosed by Khrushchev, even the most educated Russians gave themselves away. Their sense of criticism vanished, their instincts revealed them for what they are, a half-barbaric people still unacquainted with the reason and logic of the West.

We must never forget this. Guided by the instincts and emotions, the Russians can do angelic things; but they can also do diabolical things. Dostoievsky has put it well. The Russian is an idealist, who is ready to give away his life, like a Good Samaritan,* yet he can, a few

* Sometimes our guards, if they were not too closely supervised, told us to stop working, put down our tools and have a rest. Occasionally they even shared their bread and tobacco with us.

seconds later, kill the man for whom he would have sacrificed that life.

This was to me, in these last days, one of the most exciting, as well as one of the most disturbing, experiences. I really began to understand what the words "Russian soul" meant; and I realised that a shrewd and clever leader like Khrushchev, who understands this people, can lead them where he likes. He can certainly use his great power for good; but how sincere is his criticism of the old Stalinist régime? Is it simply the trick of a clever man aware of changing conditions, who knows how to turn mass opinion to his own advantage? The history of Europe in classical times, is full of demagogues, Cleon and Hyperbolus in ancient Athens, Cola di Rienzi later in Rome, down to Mussolini and Hitler in our own times; all of whom knew how to mesmerise and exploit the masses.

We Europeans did not know what to think about Khrushchev; we only knew that his coming to power had brought us relief, and for this we were heartily grateful. All concentration camp prisoners, if they are to survive, must be optimists, and we wanted to believe in Khrushchev, to see a splendid portent in him. We no longer thought in terms of a general war, which would gain us our freedom, but of a reconciliation between East and West. We hoped Khrushchev's era had inaugurated a better, happier future for us all.

Another sign of changing conditions was the education, if that is the right word, which was introduced in the form of lectures. Political officers came down and gave them, but they still contained a great deal of propaganda. These men still wanted to impress us with Russian statistics and no one, save the lecturers themselves, could have believed some of the nonsense they talked. One of the lectures which made us laugh was about the poor workers in the capitalist countries. In England, America and France, they said, workers had to queue for bread; Western workers went about in ragged clothes; they were exploited; their governments were helpless when confronted with accidents, epidemics and diseases. The lack of medicine was shameful in the West!

All this, we thought, was one of the many typically bureaucratic muddles. They had somehow got hold of material dating from the Stalin era. When they said that, in these matters, the Soviet Union was far more advanced, even those prisoners who came from the various countries of the Soviet Union, and had never seen the West, were flabbergasted. They said it was inconceivable that anyone could still talk such rubbish. "These lecturers are either swine or complete imbeciles," a Russian prisoner said to me, and then he added sadly: "If they go on being so stupid, can one ever hope things will improve?"

We told him to shrug it off as a little oddity, inseparable from a totalitarian régime, to treat it as an amiable and picturesque eccentricity.

At last we realised that we were to be repatriated, although the Hungarians were low on the list. Japanese, Turks, Persians, French, all went before us. It was not until November 1955, two and a half years after the death of Stalin, that our turn came. We were called individually to the camp office, where we had to sign a declaration of release.

The Hungarians were divided into two groups, the first being granted a *total* amnesty, that is to say that, in the eyes of the Soviet Union, they were now free men— a tacit admission that they had been wrongfully imprisoned. The second group, to which I unfortunately belonged, was being repatriated as "an act of clemency," although the Soviet Union, still considered us "guilty of crimes against the State." This distinction was to have unpleasant consequences for me when I returned to Hungary.

One morning in November, our group accompanied by only two Russian officers and two n.c.o.s were marched to the train which was to take us back to Hungary. Those who could walk, walked; the old and sick were carried on stretchers, or in horse-drawn carts. To the strains of the Hungarian national anthem, we left the world of the concentration camps. Among my companions were Miklos Csomos and Bela Kovacs.

It was a slow train and we stopped at almost every station, but we were allowed to get out and walk about the platform freely. Before leaving, we had all received new clothes without numbers and underwear; but to obtain money and buy tobacco, some of the prisoners sold them to the civilian and railway personnel on the platforms. Then they put on their old prison clothes again.

Despite the wretched condition of most of us, there was a jovial atmosphere in the train. We talked and laughed, almost like a group of schoolboys going home for the holidays. And two of the women, who had been prostitutes in Budapest, "celebrated" by offering themselves gratis to anyone who felt inclined!

When we reached Moscow, the Russian officer in charge of us said the train would wait there a day, and if we wished to visit the city, we should be back an hour before the train left. I took advantage of this extraordinary form of freedom to see the city I had, until now, known only from a prison van.

Half dazed, we wandered about the streets, staring in at shop windows most of us had not seen for ten years, thinking how wonderful it would be to go in and buy something. The Muscovites were mystified by our strange appearance and clothes, and asked us who we were. When they heard, all the good and charitable side of the Russian character came out. They were deeply emotional, some thrusting money on us, and insisting on taking us into the cafés, offering us food and drink. Queues had formed outside the food shops, and when they learned who we were, they insisted on making us go to the front. They tried to reassure us, saying that the hideous experiences we had known would never be repeated. "Papa Khrushchev will be much better," one of them said. "Have no fear! The future is bright. For you, as well as for us."

It was a very moving experience.

We also visited the huge university building where I was delighted to meet, quite by chance, a number of Hungarian students who were in Moscow on scholarships. They, too, were literally moved to tears when they heard who we were, and threw themselves into our arms. Several said they were not happy in Moscow, and would like to join us on our journey home. (But to refuse a Moscow scholarship was still, in Hungary, almost treason.) They took us to see the Kremlin, that building which had been responsible for so much of our misery; and some of us went on the Moscow underground. Other Hungarians seized the occasion, and the hospitality of the Muscovites, to get gloriously drunk. Others looked for women. Three got lost and missed the train.

We were all late in returning to the station, where we found the Russian officer commanding our escort in a state of despair. "Where have you been?" he cried. "We've had to hold up the train for you. Come on! In you get!" We could not wait for the three who had not arrived, and we gave them up for lost. But they were sent on after us by express, and rejoined us at a country station. The Russian officer in charge was delighted. "Thank God!" he cried. "How pleased I am to see you! Come and have a drink in the station restaurant! We are as happy as you are that you are all going home!" We all went in, and he paid for our drinks.

The train now went on through the famous forest of Briansk, past Gomel, Lvov, and over the Carpathians. At the Uzsok Pass we crossed the historic, thousand-year-old Hungarian frontier, which was no longer our frontier, for Soviet Russia had seized this part of Hungary in 1945. The train stopped for some minutes here, and we sang the old Hungarian national anthem, and the songs from Kurucz times which recall the greatness of our nation.

We reached Munkacs, another Hungarian town now in Russia, after midnight, but the population had heard of our arrival. They broke through the police cordon and showered us with their hard-saved little reserves of fruit and food; they embraced us, saying that however much we had suffered, we were at least going home to Hungary—while they had to remain here, under Russian rule. And all this quite openly.

We continued, and at last arrived at Zahony, the new frontier station, where we remained some hours, waiting for a Hungarian train to take us, we hoped, to Budapest. But here, on the border of our own country, one of the worst shocks of all awaited us.

20

A Prisoner in my Own Country

NOVEMBER 1955

When our train arrived that morning the Hungarian security police, the AVO, treated us with open hostility. As soon as the Russian officer had handed us over, they loaded us on to prison wagons, which were really no more than closed cattle trucks. Armed guards occupied the platforms outside, and we rolled on, prisoners again in our own country. Although Russia had sentenced and imprisoned us we had, on this last journey from the Dubrov area, been treated well by the MVD. Until now we had travelled like free people, some of us in Pullman cars. Now our own country received us as criminals.

We travelled on for an hour and a half, and at Nyiregyháza the doors were opened, and a dense cordon of AVO men, armed with tommy-guns, closed round us. They hustled us out, and drove us like sheep into what had once been the barracks of the 4th Hussars where, many years before, I had spent some weeks as a reserve officer. Now it was an AVO prison.

I have said that there were two classes of returned prisoners; those to whom the Soviet Union had granted a full amnesty, mostly ex-prisoners of war; and those like myself, who had been released only as an act of clemency, because the Soviets still considered us guilty. Of the eight hundred prisoners in this barracks, some two hundred and fifty of us were in the second category and, as I had suspected, we now began to receive very different treatment.

A number of senior AVO officers came down from Budapest to separate the sheep from the goats (Csomos and I being among the goats). I told the officer who interrogated me that I had spent almost nine years in Russian concentration camps for crimes I had not committed. But he claimed to know all about me and replied to my questions about the future with coarse and sarcastic threats. This weeding-out process continued for several days, until those of us who had not received the full amnesty had been identified. The others were given identification papers and released. We were loaded on a prison train again.

Slowly, too slowly, we advanced across the great Hungarian plain, passing Debrecen, which was recognised excitedly by some of my fellow prisoners who lived there. When we arrived at Jászbereny, shouting and cursing AVO men again took charge, herding us into an old Carmelite Convent, which was now a prison. But its religious past could not be entirely obliterated. The remains of a few frescoes, broken statues, and marble angels on the floor, proclaimed that it had once been a House of God.

We remained here for several months. It was not until February 1956 that the final phase of my prison life began. Bela Kovacs, the former Smallholder minister, and I were taken to Budapest for further interrogation (on account of his poor health, he was released after a month). I did not know that this was to be the last, for I had now come to look on life as one vast, endless interrogation.

The AVO officer who questioned me in the Fö Utca in Budapest was, I must admit, friendly. He said he admired my conduct during the war and he regretted what had since happened to me. · He only hoped that I would now be prepared to serve the cause of democracy and humanity. Several times he repeated that they needed men like me in Hungary. Our talents could be well employed in building Socialism! What were my present political views?

I said I had not changed; I was the same man I had been before my imprisonment. It was useless to expect me to support communism, after what I had seen. Its materialist philosophy was alien to me. My faith was deeply and unshakably Christian, and I would rather die than betray it. There were some other AVO officers in the room who overheard these words and they laughed. "There's nothing to be done with him," they said. "He's incurable."

Perhaps because I had spoken of my Christian faith, or perhaps because I had admitted that my sympathies lay in the West and I intended to go there, I was not released, but transferred to the national prison near the Rako-skeresztur in Budapest. In the new prison I found a number of other "Russian prisoners", as the returned Hungarian prisoners were called, who had also not received the full amnesty. Similar attempts had been made to coerce them into collaboration. At one point we told the AVO authorities that we would prefer to go back to the camps in Russia. We said we wanted to register a complaint to the Russians about their allies, the Hungarians, and their barbaric treatment of prisoners!

While I was here I fell ill, and spent the rest of my captivity in the prison hospital, being treated for a variety of minor but irritating afflictions, caused probably by my recent creosoting work—ear trouble, an abcess in the nose, inflammation of the mucous membranes.

Among the other patients in the prison hospital was

Gabor Peter, the notorious ex-head of the AVO, who had been arrested some months before and imprisoned for his Beria-like methods. His assistant, Istvan Timar, my old law colleague at the university who had been so cruel to me when I was arrested in Budapest in 1947, was also there. It was strange to look up from the yard where I was taking exercise and see Timar at a window smiling and waving, in a most friendly way. As I passed he leant down and said how pleased he was to see me back in Hungary. I shook my fist at him. The other prisoners, mostly old and sick people who were sitting on the benches by the wall, saw this and rocked with laughter.

One of the patients in the female ward of this hospital was the British journalist, Edith Bone, who has since written an account of the terror and inhuman conditions in Rakosi's Hungary. She had come to Hungary as correspondent for the *Daily Worker* several years before. When about to return to England she was arrested on the usual espionage charge (which in those days under Rakosi, was simply another way of saying, "You're an Anglo-Saxon"), and kept for years in a single cell. We did not then know who this dignified old lady was, but whenever we saw her we waved; and she gracefully acknowledged our greeting.

The first good news in hospital was about the fall of Rakosi in the summer of 1956. We felt it could not be long now before we were freed; and, in fact, one of the immediate consequences of his fall was my release in mid-October, 1956.

But before they dismissed me the AVO officers cross-questioned me and said they had not forgotten that when I was arrested I had knocked down one of their officials: I was still relatively strong and active and might easily offer further resistance to the regime.

They asked me where I would go if I were released

and I told them that my chances of beginning a new life seemed to me best in Austria, where I had relations, or in England. They then asked me if I really thought I could earn a living abroad and advised me to stay in Hungary. They went on to speak favourably of my war record and I believe it was this that eventually led to my release.

21

I Gain Freedom and Lose my Family

OCTOBER 1956

The Budapest that greeted me was very different from the one I had known nine years before. Not only did the people look different, their attitude and manner had changed. A decade of Communism had altered them beyond recognition. I was a stranger in my own land.

As I walked towards the Western railway station to take the train to Vacz, where my family were living, people stared at me, but with none of the sympathy I had felt in Moscow. An old railway porter who knew my father, and had heard of my misfortunes, was the only man in whose eyes I saw understanding. He even tried to give me money. He insisted on taking me to the buffet, where he bought me a glass of wine. His eyes filled with tears, he put his arms around me, and would not let me go.

The man in the ticket office looked at me less sympathetically when I asked for a third-class ticket. There was no such thing in the People's Democracy; I must have been away a very long time! There was only a "wooden bench class." In the train, I talked to the workers going home. When they heard where I had been, they became sympathetic, but they were also very careful what they said. I realised what it meant to live in Rakosi's Hungary.

The streets of the little town where my family lived

were dark and deserted, and when I finally found the house, my reception was as I had feared. I quickly became aware of mixed feelings. My wife was glad to see me, but she was also frightened. She had all but given up hope of seeing me again, and did not know if I had been released officially. Perhaps I had escaped! My daughters had been babies when I left, and they looked at me as if I were a stranger. Only their natural good manners were responsible for their affection and joy at seeing their father again. That night, we talked and discussed the future endlessly, and there was little sleep in the one room where the family lived.

When I suggested emigrating if we could obtain a passport, my wife said she still did not wish to leave "the tombs of her ancestors." The few days I spent with my family left me in a haze, uncertain what to do. My eyes as well as my mind, could not get used to the new environment, to the fact that I no longer lived within four prison walls, that I could go out and come in when I liked. I walked about the streets and talked to the people. Everyone was friendly, but they treated me with caution. I felt that all of them, my family included, were still frightened of what I might do or say.

A doctor friend told me to go out into the fields, in the open air, to accustom my eyes to space and distance. I went for long walks in the neighbouring hills and sat in the meadows, and tried to adapt myself to freedom. My old law colleagues told me that they were now organised in lawyers' co-operatives, and that, in the new social and economic conditions of Hungary, there was little point in my trying to take up the work again, as I had no knowledge of socialist law.

After some days I became restless and decided to see my aged father who lived in the southern part of the country, at Szentes. As my family did not wish to come abroad, I felt that after seeing him, I ought to return, and go into a factory, with a simple, perhaps a manual job, which would make me at least not a burden to them.

In the second half of that fateful October 1956, two days before the outbreak of the revolution, of which we suspected nothing, I set out for the south. I had planned to ask a friend to tell my father that I had returned, so that the shock of seeing me again would not be too great. But when I arrived, I was so eager to see him that I went straight into the room; we simply stood and stared, and then fell into one another's arms.

He had greatly aged, but he still possessed the inflexible will I had always admired, which had made him oppose both the dictatorial systems imposed on Hungary between 1920 and 1948. He had never wavered in those dangerous times; nor did he waver to-day. If he had changed physically, mentally he was as alert as ever. We spent two unforgettable days, talking, making plans for my future, and neither of us had any inkling of what lay ahead.

Then came the 23rd October, 1956, the greatest day in Hungarian history since the time of Kossuth. I took no part in the revolution, partly because of my physical condition, partly because I did not understand the immediate Hungarian past which was responsible for it: the revolt of the writers, the dismissal of Rakosi, the rehabilitation of Rajk, Gerö's speech, Titoism, and so on. I only saw with my own eyes that Hungarian democratic life began to stir again in those short halcyon days.

The municipal Government in Szentes was reorganised. It required no directives from the centre, no foreign agents, no hidden underground movement, as the Communists later claimed, to make the people rise. There was no violence, nor any need for violence. Everything was spontaneous, everywhere the most reliable, sober and honest members of the population took over the local government, and organised the collection and despatch of food to Budapest. Isolated from the rest of the country, whose railway and postal services were paralysed, they supported the ideals of the revolution wholeheartedly. How well the various classes, the workers, intellectuals, peasants and municipal officials collaborated in my father's town!

Towards the end of the first, or successful phase of the revolution, I became worried about my family and felt that I must return. After five or six days hitch-hiking in lorries I reached Pécs, where I went to the house of Bela Kovacs, whom I had not seen since we were in the Jászbereny prison together. I was most anxious to consult him, but I was informed that he had become Minister of Agriculture in the new revolutionary Government. Some workers and students had come to fetch him and he had left in such a hurry that he had not even had time to say good-bye to his family.

Still in my old prison clothes, for I had no money to buy civilian ones, and no one had any to give, I went on to Budapest, again obtaining lifts from lorries taking food to the capital.

I arrived in Budapest on the 1st November at the height of the revolution, and immediately went to the headquarters of my old party, the Smallholders, which had been resurrected. Here, I found many old friends who gave me a great welcome, and asked me to help in the party reorganisation. I was in no condition to do so yet, but I said that as soon as my health allowed, and I had arranged my family affairs, I would be pleased to.

Among the friends I found was Miklos Csomos who had been hiding the politician Bela Kovacs during the revolution. As can be imagined, Miklos was busy organising resistance groups and when he heard that I was in Budapest he rang me up. It was wonderful to hear his cheerful voice again.

"Here we are up to our necks in trouble again!" he chuckled. "We can't escape it. But if you get a chance to go West, take it. You're too ill to do much here. But I'm now completely recovered and I've been eating like a hog. I've just got Uncle Bela out of the Parliament building."

It appeared that he had organised a small group to rescue Bela Kovacs, in case he fell into the hands of the Russians again. He was also organising groups to relieve the fighters in the Killian Barracks.*

Then came the early hours of 4th November, when the Russian tanks invaded Budapest, and we heard Imre Nagy's radio appeal to the country and to the West. He spoke with calm and dignity, and we listened, still half-hoping that some miracle might save us. Foreign radio stations such as Radio Free Europe in Munich encouraged the Hungarians to fight on; they were full of enthusiasm for our revolution. The B.B.C. was more moderate; it gave accurate news bulletins, and said that in the U.N.O. the General Assembly had been convoked. This did not mean a great deal, but we felt that the West must accept this opportunity and send us help.

The fighting continued, and no foreign help came. I was in one of the houses where the freedom fighters returned with their wounded, the first harbingers of yet another tragedy that was about to strike the Hungarian people. Then we knew that we had been left alone to fight. The free world was looking the other way.

When it was clear that the revolt was about to be crushed, more friends told me that I would be in danger,

*Much later, after the revolution collapsed, Miklos managed to escape to Switzerland and he is now practising as a dentist in Basel. We still write to each other from time to time.

after my years of imprisonment in Russia, and that I should be accused of taking part in the rising. I must escape to the West. I hesitated at first, refusing to leave my family and the home I had only just come back to. But they knew Hungary better than I did and insisted. I therefore sent a message to my wife begging her to come with me and to bring our children, explaining my reasons. But she felt she could not.

Russian troops were now invading the country from Czechoslovakia, occupying the entire Austrian frontier region, and we thought it would be useless to try to escape in that direction. But we then heard on the wireless that new groups of refugees were daily crossing the Austrian frontier and sending back radio messages from Vienna that they had arrived safely.

I set off with a couple of friends and in two days, hiding from the Russian tanks, we reached Kapuvar on Lake Ferto. The local guides knew the best crossing points into Austria and were going to and fro, day and night, with refugees. Three farmers, helped by some Hungarian frontier guides, took us to a bridge, over the canal which divided the countries, but when we arrived we found that it had been blown up. Exhausted, we waded across into Austria.

The Austrian frontier guards received us hospitably, gave us food and drink, and took us to a village where the school had been turned into a reception centre, with a kitchen and dormitories. No one should ever forget the kindness of the Austrian people at this time. I telephoned my relations in Vienna, who were amazed, but deeply moved, to learn that I had come alive out of that hell on earth in Russia.

After only two hours in this friendly little village, my relations came by car and took me to Vienna where I stayed with my sister-in-law, Baroness Herbert Reichlin-Meldegg. For two whole days I slept.

Then I went to my previous employers, the British Embassy in Vienna. I told them that I had worked for them in 1947; that for this I had been arrested and sentenced by the Russians to twenty-five years' hard labour as a British spy; and that during all these years of imprisonment I had prayed God that I might come back alive and see them again.

They looked at me suspiciously, for none of them had been there in 1947. They exchanged glances and then one of them went to his superior to report that a strange Hungarian, who said he had been imprisoned in Russia as a British spy, had arrived from Budapest, claiming British support. An older man came out and looked at me curiously. I told him what had happened; and he seemed to believe me, for he asked me to wait while he telephoned London.

Three quarters of an hour later he returned and said that everything I had said had been confirmed. I could leave for London on the first refugee transport. I did not even have time to take leave of my relations in Vienna, because at dawn the next day I was on an aeroplane bound for London, with the first group of Hungarians to get away, forty-seven of us. I was still wearing my Russian prison uniform when I landed near London, at Blackbushe airport.

THE END

APPENDIX

The Death Sentence in Russia

Severe as my sentence to twenty-five years' hard labour was, I was lucky to have it passed in 1948. In any other year I would have been executed for my alleged "high treason and espionage." "Crimes against the State" had been capital offences in Communist law from 1919 to 1947. Then, in that year, not long before my trial, capital punishment was abolished. This lasted only a little over a year, until 1949, so that my case coincided with the period of "clemency."

The reason for this, I later discovered, was that the Russian Communists, having just won a war, felt secure, and wished to show the rest of the world, where capital punishment still existed, particularly the Western democracies of Britain and America, how much more "humane" they were. For capital punishment has, strangely enough, always been repugnant to the Slav mentality. As I was to learn, if for some reason an execution had to take place, it never did so with all the hideous Western panoply of gallows, hangman, guillotine, electric chair, etc. The Russians preferred to send the condemned man out into the wood with a posse of soldiers, one of whom shoots him in the head from behind when he is not expecting it.

I must add too, to support my theory about the attitude of the Russians towards capital punishment that, if it has existed for political and state crimes, it has never existed for civil crimes. (It has only just been introduced for civil crimes for the first time in Soviet history, in 1961.) The most sanguinary murders in our camp were punished with only a few months' imprisonment.

Why then was capital punishment for "crimes against the State" restored in 1949, shortly after my condemnation? The reason I believe is, that by 1947, the Russians felt so secure against Western espionage that they were not frightened of it. The Western Allies had not wanted to offend their ally while relations were good immediately after the war, and they had undertaken no espionage in Russia. Then in 1948 came the Berlin blockade and the beginning of the cold war. The Western powers found Russian espionage increasing so much in their own countries, that they had to resort to it themselves. The Soviet occupied countries soon found an increasing number of Western agents (hence their suspicion of me), and they finally reintroduced the extreme penalty, to discourage them. As far as I know, the death penalty for these crimes still exists in Soviet Russia; but as soon as the Communists feel secure, I am sure they will abolish it again.

NORWAY
SWEDEN
FINLAND
Leningrad
UNION O
ESTONIA
LATVIA
LITHUANIA
R.S.F.S.R.
WHITE
RUSSIA
Bryansk
Ry
Baltic Sea
E. GERMANY
POLAND
UKRAINE
L'vov
CZECHOSLOVAKIA
AUSTRIA
Vienna
Baden
Budapest
HUNGARY
RUMANIA
Sea
YUGOS

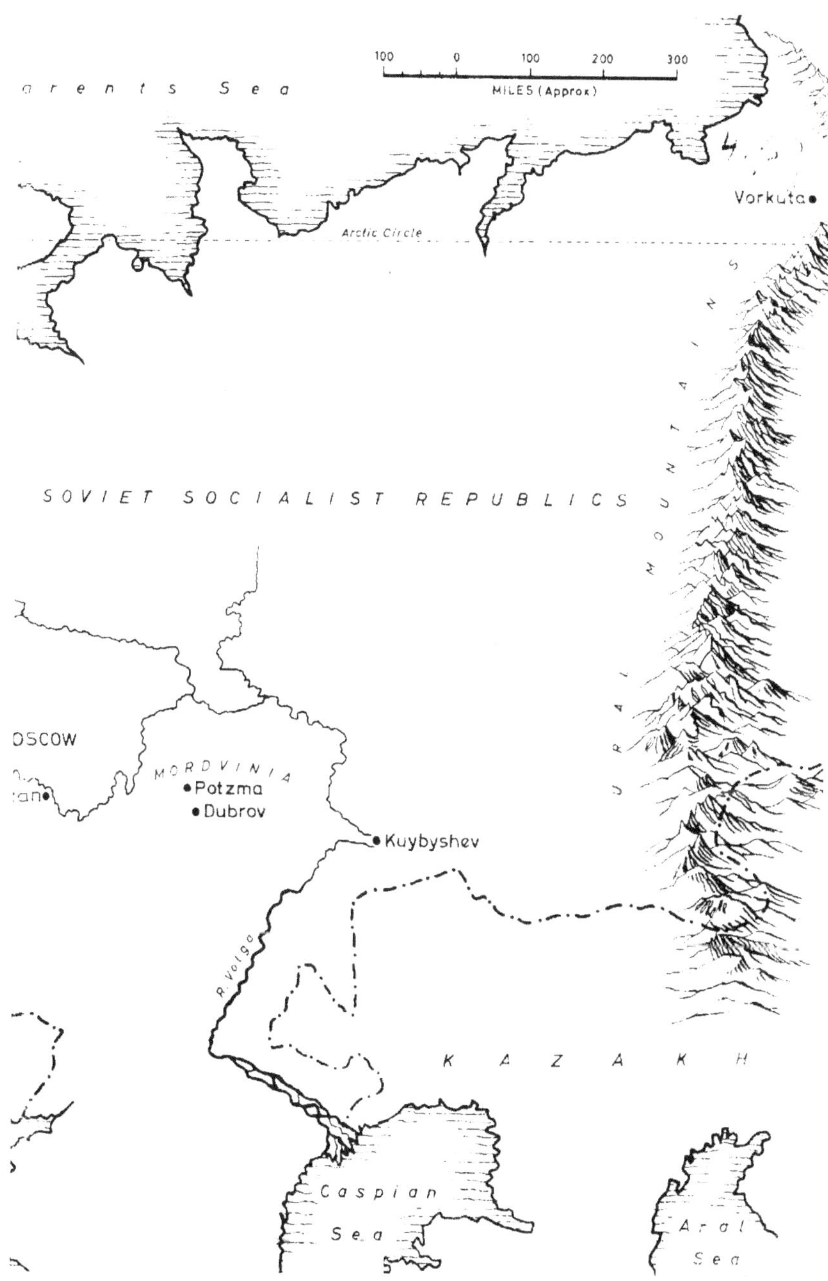

arents Sea
100   0   100   200   300
MILES (Approx)
Vorkuta
Arctic Circle
SOVIET SOCIALIST REPUBLICS
URAL MOUNTAINS
MOSCOW
MORDVINIA
Potzma
Dubrov
Kuybyshev
R. Volga
KAZAKH
Caspian Sea
Aral Sea